From
Surviving
to Thriving

From Surviving to Thriving

TRANSFORMING YOUR CAREGIVING JOURNEY

Amy S. D'Aprix, MSW, PhD

SECOND LIFE PRESS

CHAPEL HILL, NORTH CAROLINA

From Surviving to Thriving: Transforming Your Caregiving Journey

Copyright © 2008 Amy S. D'Aprix

PUBLISHED BY

Second Life Press
1289 Fordham Boulevard, Suite 125
Chapel Hill, North Carolina 27514
www.caregiverscoach.com

DESIGNED AND PRODUCED BY

Boulder Bookworks LLC, Boulder, Colorado USA
www.boulderbookworks.com

First Edition

ISBN: 978-0-9801731-0-9

Library of Congress Control Number: 2007910063

Printed in Canada

DEDICATION

This book is dedicated to Warren and Alice D'Aprix, my parents and greatest teachers. The last few years of their lives were filled with many challenges, yet they lived to the end with determination, grace, humor, compassion, and dedication to each other. They left me the greatest legacy parents could leave a child: the awareness that our ability to feel and express love and compassion is all that really matters in life.

Contents

ACKNOWLEDGMENTS

This book moved from idea to reality because of the hard work and dedication of many people, most notably Karen Monaco and Carol Kohn, whose creative energies are reflected on nearly every page. Ruth Ann Uhl also helped bring this book to completion by stepping in at the last stages and providing organization and renewed energy. I also want to express my gratitude to both Vicki Field and Jay Koebele, who have worked side by side with me since the inception of The Caregivers' Coach. Without them, I would never have had the courage, energy, or ability to begin The Caregivers' Coach or write this book.

Who is Dr. Amy?

 Dr. Amy—the Caregivers' Coach, as she is affectionately known by caregivers—is a highly sought-after speaker throughout North America on the topics of aging and caregiving.

As a gerontological social worker, she began working with seniors and families over twenty years ago. In addition to her extensive academic and professional background she was a caregiver to her own parents for over a decade.

You can find many free tips, tools, and strategies to assist you with your caregiving journey—including a free caregiver tip of the day—at www.caregiverscoach.com.

Introduction

Why I Wrote This Book

My mother was a wonderfully energetic person; she never sat still. Even in retirement, she was always on the go. She became a racewalker and a swimmer in the Senior Games and won several gold medals. Mom loved people, and they loved her—everything about her, especially the laugh you could hear a block away!

Then, when Mom was just 69, the unimaginable happened. She suffered a stroke that left her severely disabled. We were told it was a miracle she survived. My mother, who always lived life on the move, was partially paralyzed, could barely talk, and had limited cognitive capacity. In the blink of an eye, she was confined to a wheelchair, and feeding herself was the extent of her abilities. After a year rehabilitating in a long-term care facility my mother returned home, where she lived for another seven years. Because of her physical and mental limitations, my mother required nearly constant care. She attended an adult day care program and had home care services both morning and evening. Although she had severe disabilities, my mother never lost her smile, sense of humor, or will to live. I believe that the love she felt from her family, friends, and professional caregivers during her last years helped make those years some of the best of her life.

My father lived for three years after my mother's death. During those years, he was in relatively good health and needed only occasional assistance. In the last year of his life he began to decline slowly at first, then more rapidly in the last months. My father became my teacher. By his example, he taught me the devotion of a caregiver as he looked after my mother. He showed me the struggle of finding his purpose, without his life partner. And I watched him suffer, with dignity, his own health challenges.

Being a caregiver for my parents transformed my life in many and positive ways, but I was luckier than many. I had over a decade of professional experience as a social worker. I began my career as a home care social worker, helping families find care for their frail or disabled older relatives and helping them work through emotional and family issues that come along in those situations. Later, as part of a geriatric assessment team, I worked with patients with Alzheimer's disease and their families. Following that, I taught social work students at both graduate and undergraduate levels.

Even with my background, caregiving was a challenge. I remember asking myself, "If caregiving is this challenging for me, what is it like for caregivers without my experience?" I wondered how people managed without knowledge of the health and long-term care systems. Where did they turn for help? How did they deal with the emotional roller coaster? How did they manage time and tasks and marshal the help of friends and family? The questions kept coming, often in the middle of the night.

The answers did not come as quickly as the questions. Soon, though, it became clear to me that I could bring my academic training, my professional experience, and my personal experience as a caregiver together to help others on their caregiving journeys. As our population ages, many of us are likely to be called to provide care for an elderly relative or friend or to support someone else. Caregiving, I've learned firsthand, is not something we must simply endure—hoping to survive—caregiving and the loved ones we care for provide an experience we can grow from, learn to appreciate, and even come to savor. It is an experience that can transform our lives for the better.

Why Should You Read This Book?

Many caregivers don't identify themselves as such. They say, "I'm not a caregiver, I just pop in and check on Mom twice a week and take her to get groceries and to the doctor" or "I'm not a caregiver, I just started paying the bills and running errands after my aunt's vision got so bad." Who, then, is a caregiver? *A caregiver is one who does anything at all that helps keep an older person independent or improves his or her quality of life.* Thus, the adult child who lives far away but calls several times a week to offer emotional support to an aging parent is a caregiver. So is the son who takes care of his parents' home repairs and yard work, and the woman who checks each morning to see if her neighbor's blinds have been opened so she knows her friend is awake and safe. And, of course, the wife caring for her husband with Alzheimer's disease or the husband caring for his wife with cancer are both caregivers.

There is a second part to caregiving, beyond looking after someone else. It is looking after yourself—what I call *caregiver wellness.* Caregivers can easily sacrifice their own health and well-being without even being aware they are doing it. The focus on providing care for an aging relative often overshadows one's need to take care of him- or herself. Research on caregiving has shown that neglecting one's self has serious consequences. It even has a name, *caregiver syndrome.* Dr. Jean Posner, a neuropsychiatrist in Baltimore, Maryland, defines caregiver syndrome as a "debilitating condition brought on by unrelieved, constant caring for a person with a chronic illness or dementia" (www.CNN.com/health).

So, if you feel responsible for the well-being of an older adult *and* you are concerned about your own well-being, then this book is for you. This book will give you help and ideas about attending to your inner life and your relationships, including your relationship with your aging relative and the people with whom you live, work, and interact. The articles and stories are designed to inspire you, comfort you, guide you, and, most important, help you develop a positive perspective on caregiving.

How This Book Is Organized

Chapter 1 lays the groundwork for this book. I describe my philosophy of *transformational caregiving* and provide some insights into how caregiving can positively transform your life. This philosophy has been informed by my academic training, my professional and personal experience, and the many caregivers with whom I have worked.

Circle 1: Self-Care and Caregiving

Caregiver wellness is easy to talk about but may be hard to achieve. Just how do you take good care of yourself while providing excellent care to someone else? Begin by developing positive, supportive relationships with family and friends and even with casual acquaintances. Like the pebble dropped in the pond, let your relationships reach well beyond your inner circle. Think, for a moment, about the ripples that pebble creates on the water; they radiate out in concentric circles. The inner circle represents your relationship with yourself. If you ignore self-care you are ignoring the most important aspect of caregiver wellness. Yet we see all too often that this is the relationship the caregiver nurtures least. In Circle 1, I'll offer you practical ideas and ways to take care of yourself on this caregiving journey.

Circle 2: The Caregiver's Relationship with the Care Recipient

The next, larger circle encompasses the relationship with the person for whom you are providing care, the focus of your time and energy. There are many relationship challenges that accompany the physical and mental changes your loved one is experiencing. There are also many, many opportunities for a renewed relationship with him or her: opportunities to heal hurts in the relationship, enjoy precious time together, create new memories, and even say goodbye to someone you love. Circle 2 articles provide new perspectives on that relationship.

Circle 3: Relationships with Family and Close Friends

The third circle radiating from your center focuses on relationships with family and close friends. Family can be both the greatest source of support and the greatest source of our struggles during caregiving. In Circle 3 you will find suggestions for creating and sustaining more harmonious relationships with family members, as well as tips for strengthening relationships with close friends.

Circle 4: Relationships with the Greater Community

Circle 4 reaches all the other people you regularly interact with, in the workplace, community groups, your children's school, and faith communities. While these people may be more acquaintances than close friends, they still have an impact on your sense of well-being. In Circle 4 you will find ways to negotiate these relationships, so they become supportive and not additional sources of stress.

Circle 5: Working with Professionals

The fifth circle, farthest from your center, considers relationships with all professionals with whom you interact while caregiving: primary care doctors and specialists, nurses, home care workers, nursing home staff, and rehabilitation therapists. As a caregiver you will most likely find it necessary to interact with professionals who have not been part of your daily activities. These professionals often play vital roles in providing needed information, support, and services. And the relationships may not always be easy. Circle 5 offers concrete strategies for maximizing support and minimizing frustration when dealing with professionals.

Chapter 7 closes the book by discussing caregiving as a transformational experience, recognizing the impact your loved one continues to have in your life long after he or she has left this world. It describes honoring your loved one's journey and keeping him or her alive in your memory.

For free tips and tools to assist and inspire you on your caregiving journey, please visit www.caregiverscoach.com. While you are there I invite you to share your thoughts, ideas, wisdom, and humor about caregiving by choosing "share caregiver wisdom."

CHAPTER ONE

Transforming Caregiving from Surviving to Thriving

No one would ever have crossed the ocean if he could have gotten off the ship in the storm.

CHARLES KETTERING

IT IS LIKELY THAT THE EARLY EXPLORERS felt overwhelmed, especially during rough weather. They may have wished they could go home as they were being tossed about by wild storms. But imagine what they would have missed—the adventure of exploration, experiences they couldn't even have imagined, and a new life in a new land.

As a caregiver, you may have wished that this journey was a little easier, or at least that you could just turn this ship around and go back to your old life. Perhaps, though, you want more than mere survival, you want to benefit from the whole experience.

I believe that caregiving will not simply benefit you; it will transform you. This notion of transformation is thrown around a lot these days, but it is an important concept for caregivers. Transformation means that you are changed in a permanent way. A butterfly, for example, cannot return to the cocoon and resume life as a caterpillar. Neither can you go back to being the person you were before you became a caregiver, nor would you want to. The caregiving experience can be rich and rewarding and change you in unexpected ways.

You might ask: if caregiving for an aging loved one can be a positive, transformational experience, why do I feel like I'm struggling just to make it through the day? The truth is that when you are in the midst of caregiving it is unlikely that you are focused on what a wonderful opportunity caregiving provides for transforming your life. Instead, you are likely consumed with the tasks of caregiving, of trying to keep your life in balance, and in coping with the barrage of emotions that are common for caregivers.

Often caregiving is complicated by the fact that caregivers add these responsibilities to an already full life. To complicate things further, many people have no advance notice they are going to become caregivers. Instead, they receive a phone call that their loved one has had a major fall, heart attack, stroke, or something else that has quickly and dramatically impacted his or her functioning. Unlike parents who get nine months to prepare for their new role, caregivers may not even get nine minutes!

For all of these reasons, it is very important to step back from time to time to regain your perspective and recognize the many ways caregiving can enrich your life. One of the ways that caregiving can positively impact your life is by allowing you to revisit your past. You may find that you spend much more time with your loved one and with other family members than you have in years. This may be challenging, while at the same time it may allow you to see those relationships in new ways, to heal past wounds, and to form stronger bonds. Many, many caregivers look back on this as a healing time, one that allowed them to release the past and to move forward less burdened.

Through caregiving, you may also get a peek into the future and an opportunity to contemplate the end of your own life. As uncomfortable as that might be, it is nearly impossible not to think about it as you watch someone you love grow older and die. A person who is transformed by the caregiving experience often views caregiving as the wake-up call needed to examine his or her own life and determine if it has meaning. You may realize that you are not satisfied or content and decide to shift the focus of your thoughts, energy, and time.

The transformation I'm talking about does not happen magically. In fact, you may not recognize it until after your caregiving has ended. People who are transformed by caregiving still must work through all the difficulties and challenges. Actually, it is *because* of these challenges, not *in spite* of them, that transformation takes place. It is by facing these challenges head on, and by stepping back from time to time to integrate the lessons that these challenges offer, that you will find your life changing. The end result is that caregivers who are transformed by the experience often see this as the beginning of a new path, one that brings more joy and contentment and resonates more closely with their values and dreams. Could there be a greater gift someone receives from caregiving?

My hope for you is that you emerge from your caregiving experience transformed. That you become a person who lives your life in a way that gives you joy and contentment, in harmony with what you value and what gives your life meaning. I hope that you emerge with the awareness that even when someone lives to be very old, life is very short.

The articles and related stories in this book are from caregivers and provide you with practical strategies and support as you deal with the emotions that I expect you will experience. Please recognize that you are not alone, that all emotions are real and important, and that there is support available. If by reading this book you recognize that you need more support than is offered here, I encourage you to seek out a professional coach or counselor.

CHAPTER TWO

Circle 1: **Self-Care and Caregiving**

*The time to relax is when you don't
have time for it.*

SIDNEY J. HARRIS

CAREGIVERS OFTEN GO TO EXTRAORDINARY LENGTHS
to provide nurturing, love, and emotional and physical
support to an aging relative in need. In addition to caring for
an aging family member, many caregivers also provide care to
children or other family members. Yet there is one person who
often gets neglected in all of this caregiving: the caregiver
herself!

We all know that you can't get water from an empty well.
Despite that, it is quite common for caregivers to ignore their
own needs for long periods of time while providing care for an
aging relative. This may be necessary during a crisis or on a
short-term basis, but it is not an effective long-term strategy.
Caregivers who ignore their own needs on an ongoing basis
often end up sick or too exhausted to provide care for their
loved ones. That is why this is the inner circle, the core of the
concentric circles. Clearly good self-care is the circle that all
other circles radiate out from.

The solution to poor, or no, self-care is to first recognize
its importance and then to creatively find ways to get your
needs met. In the articles and stories in this chapter you will

find tips, tools, and strategies to help you do just that—meet YOUR needs. Remember the goal is caregiver wellness, which means taking good care of yourself while taking good care of someone else.... So here's to you!

Italy vs. Holland

Imagine you spent your whole life dreaming about and planning a trip to Italy. As a child you got the idea that you wanted to visit Italy, and you could never get it out of your mind. As you got older you could imagine yourself sitting in a small café in Rome enjoying pasta and local wine. You saw yourself driving through the Italian countryside and visiting different cities. You studied Italian and saved every extra dollar for your dream trip.

Finally, the day arrived; you were leaving for Italy. As the plane landed, you heard the flight attendant announce, "Ladies and gentlemen, welcome to Holland." How could this be? You were going to Italy; how did you get highjacked to Holland?

Becoming a caregiver can be a little like ending up in Holland when your heart was set on Italy. You, no doubt, have a picture of how your life is supposed to unfold, almost a life script. You may plan your professional life step by step, or you may have a particular period, like retirement, that you've scripted. Then, something happens that completely alters the scene—loss of a job, end of a marriage, a parent or spouse who needs care. You might say that you've just gone from Italy to Holland. It happens to most of us at least once.

Some caregivers easily give up or postpone activities that have become impossible given their new responsibilities, while others simply cannot let go of what they feel they are missing. Can you, then, learn to appreciate the Holland in your life and let go of your dream of Italy, at least temporarily? The extent to which you are able to do it could determine your level of enjoyment and peace of mind.

It is normal to grieve for what you have lost, be that a loved one or a way of life. The key is not to let that grief take charge. You choose how long grief rules your life—how long you keep wishing you were in Rome. The danger of hanging onto a dream that has changed is that you miss the joy and the beauty of the new experience. And, while you might not have chosen your caregiving situation, if you can be open to the new landscape, you may find that caregiving does have beauty and value of its own.

Harry and I had such plans for our years in retirement—travel, gardening, reconnecting with old friends. Then Harry suffered a stroke, and I became his primary caregiver. Because the stroke permanently limited his walking and speaking, I knew I had to find a way to deal with my loss of our planned future, a constructive way to live with what was.

I turned to professionals and friends for ideas and then I set off on my journey, quite a different one than we had originally visualized together. It wasn't always easy, and in the beginning I struggled to keep my new perspective in place. But, as I lived each day with Harry, I found new activities, small trips to our favorite gardens, and friends who came to visit us rather than our taking long trips.

My landscape has changed from my original vision, but it still holds many wonderful moments. By not clinging to my feelings of loss, I was able to move forward and participate fully in what I have now.

Mary, 73

The Choice Is Yours

One of the hot spots of stress in caregiving is the feeling that you have no choice about being a caregiver. People who choose to be caregivers still experience stress, but not to the extent of those who feel that caregiving has been dropped in their laps.

When you choose your own actions, you feel in control of your life, and the more control you feel, the less stress you feel. So, one way to decrease your caregiving stress is to change your perspective and to view caregiving as a choice.

William felt the role of caregiver was definitely not a choice but rather something foisted upon him. It didn't mean he didn't love his elderly father; it meant he didn't feel it was his own decision to take on the responsibility. He had been the family member available and the one most involved with his father. He was the default caregiver.

If you, like William, are feeling coerced, there is good news. You can stop, reexamine the situation, and make a new choice at any time. Here are some ideas about how to increase your sense of choice and gain control of your caregiving experience.

Stop keeping score. If you are the default caregiver or the person who lives the closest, determine what you want to do as a caregiver, regardless of what others do or don't do. Pretend for a moment there are no other family members. Then, list the caregiving tasks you are willing to do without resentment. You may find that your list doesn't differ much from what you are actually doing. You may find the reason you resent doing these tasks is that there are other family members who could be helping but are not. How does this list making reduce stress? By helping you remember that you choose to do these things.

Ask others to do more. When you do this you must detach yourself from the outcome. Remember that you are responsible for your own behavior and that only you can control it. So, make a choice to ask for help, then do your best to accept the response, whatever it may be. *Adopt a one-day-at-a-time philosophy.* Most caregivers will say they can easily handle their responsibilities today. It is tomorrow that gets scary. So, today focus on what you can choose to do and control, and let tomorrow come as it may. Spending your energy anticipating the unknown only adds stress today. *Make conscious choices.* Sometimes simply saying to yourself, "I choose to be a caregiver for Mother today," can remind you that you have made the choice. It is a reminder that ultimately you are free to choose the intentions and actions that control your life.

I never considered that I had a choice about being my mother's caregiver. She has dementia, and I am the primary family caregiver. Once I realized that I could see this role as something I really wanted to do, sort of an attitude switch, my whole perspective changed. I was no longer angry with my sister and brother once I decided to make a task list—one for each of us. Keeping in mind that this is my choice allows me to appreciate the many benefits of this time I have with my mother.

Patricia, 53

Make Anger an Ally

Regardless of where we live, we are subject to the whims of nature. Will it be too windy to fish? Will that hurricane give us any trouble this week? Will too much or too little rain affect our crops? Family caregivers experience similar situations, inner hurricanes of anger, storms of frustration.

Most of us have been taught not to express our anger. You may feel you need to bury it, pretend it is not there, or push it down with some distraction. Taken to an extreme, your anger can turn inward and become dark depression. Even more troubling is that unexpressed anger can eat away at your happiness and physical well-being over time.

In spite of a lifetime's teaching, consider for a moment that anger could actually be an important ally. Here's why.

Caregiving is all about change. Your own life changes, often dramatically and rapidly. You will witness changes in your loved one's physical and mental abilities, which, in turn, trigger additional changes in his or her habits. And, with any kind of change, it is human nature to experience a full range of emotions known as the grief cycle. For example, after the initial shock of bad news or a significant loss, the brain protects itself by means of shock and then denial. Sometimes denial goes on for a long period of time, thus sapping more and more energy from your ability to deal with what's next.

Anger is a natural part of the grief cycle. It is associated with an urge to attack, creating specific physiological changes that enable action. Anger creates focus by narrowing our thinking. The passion of anger feels better than the quiet desperation of helplessness and depression. When we listen, anger can illuminate our needs and animate our wills. Anger can power us to say and do what is needed.

Consider the possibility that anger is a positive step in the journey of loss, letting go, and completion. It is the bridge between the past and the present so that you can find solutions that move you forward. In acknowledging anger, you come into the present. It is often a signal that you are moving toward acceptance and a new beginning.

So cherish your health and happiness by letting anger have its way with you, in the right time and place. Find a safe friend or coach to help you find the words for your anger; he or she can help you get to the truth beneath it. Although it's not wise to make decisions in anger, it is helpful to be open to what those angry feelings may be telling you. What a paradox. Anger can be an ally for keeping your best self available to your loved one.

⟶⟵

I've always prided myself on being composed and in control of my emotions. I felt anger was not something either helpful or desirable. Then, my wife, Elaine, was diagnosed with Alzheimer's. As I watched her deteriorate, I wanted to scream and curse, but I held it all in.

My friend Paul sensed what I was going through and suggested talking with a professional. He said, "John, you are going through a major and demanding change, no wonder you are angry and maybe that is all right." At first, I was reluctant, but I relented and felt like a veil was lifting. I learned that anger was telling me something, and I began to listen. I started running again and talking to people I had been avoiding. The more I acknowledged my anger the more I was able to accept what was ahead for Elaine and me.

I now see anger as my "buddy," and I listen carefully. Anger has allowed me to face what needs to be done for my wife, and I know that having feelings means I am alive and fighting for her. I've turned the tables, and now anger works for me, not against me.

John, 57

Just Ask—Ask, Ask, Ask!

Early one Saturday morning Susan took a taxi to the airport and asked the taxi driver to stop at the bank so she could make an important deposit into her checking account. Susan was leaving town for a week and needed to make the deposit so that her automatic payments would be covered. The bank was closed, so Susan had stepped to the bank's ATM and reached for a deposit envelope. There were none. With time passing and in a mild panic she asked the taxi driver if he might have an envelope. Indeed he did and not just a plain envelope but a bank deposit envelope! With great relief, Susan made her deposit, returned to the taxi, and was off to the airport.

"What a long shot that you'd have an envelope," she said to the driver, "I don't know why I thought to ask."

"When you need something in life," the kind and very wise taxi driver said, "you just have to ask for it—ask, ask, ask! Someone will always have what you need, but you have to ask." He repeated this to Susan several times, and she quickly saw the lesson, much bigger than a deposit envelope.

How many times have you had to do things yourself simply because you didn't ask? How many times was there someone nearby who could have made your life easier if only you'd thought to ask them?

Feeling burdened is a common emotion experienced by caregivers. You may have felt, at one time or another, like there is much more to do then you could possibly get done. But, you may not have asked for help. Or, if you do ask for help, it may always be from the same few people you always go to for help.

What if, just for today, you asked more freely for help with things so that you were less burdened by caregiving, by life in general? You don't even have to ask for help with the caregiving tasks, you can ask for help with other things that add to your burden—laundry, house cleaning, projects at work.

Remember Susan's taxi ride, and become more aware that all you have to do is ask for help—ask, ask, ask! Often you will get what you need. People generally want to be helpful; perhaps you're not giving them the opportunity.

—◆—

I've always had a hard time asking for help from people outside my own family. One day I was feeling particularly overwhelmed by all the things I had to do to help my elderly father. It was autumn and the leaves in my yard hadn't been raked and were piling up all over the place. I hadn't slept well the night before, and I just didn't feel like I had the energy to clean up those leaves.

That very morning, I had heard an announcement on the radio about a local group called A Helping Hand, *but I wasn't sure what they did. I was desperate, so I called the number and explained my needing help with yard work.*

I learned that A Helping Hand *was comprised of students taking part in a community service project. Before I knew it, two cars arrived with eight young women full of fun and good spirit. They raked and bagged the leaves and seemed to enjoy doing it. They thanked me for the opportunity to help me with that chore. I was so delighted that I invited them back in the spring to help with planting and mulching. I got a resounding Yes! This one experience opened my eyes to the help that is available, and all I had to do was ask.*

Jacquelyn, 47

Recharging Your Batteries

Caregivers regularly hear about the importance of taking a break from their caregiving responsibilities in order to recharge, renew, and refresh. This is so critical that it bears repeating. Sometimes, though, it is hard to come up with practical ways to do it.

Every time Alice heard "recharge your battery," she would just sigh and think, "I have no time for that." In truth, Alice learned she didn't need much time, five or ten minutes was all it took to change her whole outlook. A week away was out of the question, so Alice's goal became to create mini-breaks.

The following list is a mixture of ideas—some you can do in a few minutes and others take a little longer, and a few you can do in brief captured moments while you are caregiving. Scheduling regular mini-breaks for yourself—at least three times a week—can help relax you and can certainly reduce tension. Creativity, more than time, is one key to feeling refreshed. Here are a dozen to spark your own creative ideas:

1. Give yourself 15 minutes, and, to the extent possible, turn off everything that makes noise, including your cell phone. Sit quietly, close your eyes, and picture yourself in one of your favorite spots—on the beach, walking a mountain trail, playing with your dog.

2. Take a walk in nature or go for a drive in the country.

3. Work in your, or someone else's, garden; feel connected to the earth.

4. Read a book or magazine into which you can escape.

5. Have a massage.

6. Listen to soothing music.

7. Draw on your own hobbies. Knit, crochet, sew, cook, or work on your favorite craft.

8. Go to bed early, sleep a little late, or take a midday catnap.

9. Relax, and pet your dog or cat.

10. Start planning your dream vacation, knowing its time will come.

11. Have lunch with a friend.

12. Do something spontaneous with your family; go out for the evening with your spouse or partner.

I'm a social worker, and I had forgotten that in order to be an effective caregiver for Dad I had to take some time and focus on my own mental health. I was reminded when my daughter said, "I know what you do for Granddad, but what do you do for yourself?" I made up my mind then and there that I would do one thing just for myself every day.

Between work and caregiving, I don't have much free time so my breaks are small ones, maybe five minutes to go somewhere by myself and sit quietly. It never fails to amaze to me how these mini-breaks can release some of the tension and renew my spirit. I feel refreshed when I go back to helping Dad. Tomorrow, my neighbor is coming to be with Dad, and I am going to have lunch with a dear friend. We've agreed to talk of nothing but gardening.

Adele, 48

Finding the Humor

Have you ever come across that sign that says "May you always see the humor in the human condition"? As a caregiver, you may be saying to yourself, "There's nothing funny about my situation."

This mindset has been referred to by many as *terminal seriousness*, and there is a cure! You can transplant your overly serious perspective with a more light-hearted approach. Here are some ways to do it.

► View your situation through the eyes of a child. Small children, as you no doubt know, do not suffer from terminal seriousness. They can see the silly side of any situation. So invite that childlike perspective to come out and play.

► Actively seek out the humor and the joy in life, even in the most difficult situations. Doctors, firefighters, police, and others who daily face traumatic situations often develop the ability to see something funny in the moment, when we might only see sadness. We can all benefit from recognizing that even in dark moments there may be something that can trigger the funny bone enough to keep us from sinking—look hard for it.

► Create silliness in your life. The humorist Loretta LaRoche encourages people to be silly in their day-to-day lives as a way of keeping stress at bay. Take the annoyances of life and put a humorous spin on them. It is a wonderful art, one well worth learning. Today, let yourself be silly. Start small if silliness seems silly to you. You may be amazed at how your perspective will change.

► Ask yourself, "If I were to die tomorrow, would this really matter?" If the answer is no, strive to let it go! Eliminate the possibility of future regret by promising yourself you will enjoy life—just as it is now. This doesn't mean you have to change your location or situation, just your perspective.

► Take Scarlett O'Hara's approach and decide to "worry about that tomorrow." Tell yourself that for today you are going to find something to laugh about. You've probably noticed that most things you worry about don't ever happen anyway, so there is real wisdom in postponing worry. If you *must* worry, then schedule a time to worry and then limit yourself to that time. By postponing and limiting your worrying, you will have more time for joy and happiness.

Do you recognize the symptoms of terminal seriousness in your caregiving situation? Give some of these suggestions a try. Once you've made room for joy, you may find you enjoy your caregiving role more.

—————

My husband, Leonard, has been ill for so long we can hardly remember the good times we used to have. Our conversations seemed to focus on his illness and the doctors and the medications.

Once we realized that our life had only one focus, we made a pact to find at least one thing to laugh about every single day. We decided to get really silly, and we got some old Three Stooges movies; we enjoy their foolishness. One evening, Leonard surprised me by pulling out our old album of pictures taken when we were just dating. We couldn't stop laughing at our hair and clothes.

We have a competition of sorts now to see who can think up something funny and get the other one laughing. It's been a great relief for both of us to stop dwelling so much on the illness.

Gertrude, 76

Guilty Feelings

Dealing with feelings—expected and unexpected, good and bad—is routine for caregivers. Some soldier on through the emotion, but others can't. Guilty feelings are quite common and often the most difficult for caregivers to deal with.

May, who is 78, sometimes wonders how long her husband with dementia will live. John, a middle-aged businessman, has cared for his declining, elderly father for five years. These two caregivers can understand the two sides of chronic illness. The good side is that their loved ones have lived so long, perhaps exceeding the doctors' expectations. The downside is that, because their loved ones have lived so long, they, themselves, have become weary caregivers.

In these situations, you may wonder just how long it will go on. You may perceive that your loved one's quality of life has diminished, or, like May, you've lost a sense of connection to him or her because of the illness or condition. Then, you might feel guilty about even having such thoughts and feelings.

When these feelings overwhelm you, take a moment to stop and put things in perspective. Here are some ideas on how to do that.

► Forgive yourself. Caregiving is tough work and it is more than natural to want it to end, to get back to your own life as fully as possible. These feelings may indicate that you need to take better care of yourself. Take a break. Ask for some help. Get out and relax, and try to forget about the illness for a while.

► Forgive your loved one. If she has mental capacity, she is probably aware of the wonderful care you are providing. Chances are she will be happier if you can figure out ways to get relief and take some time for yourself. You may not be the only one feeling guilt in this situation.

► When the caregiving experience goes on for a long time, you will need to continually balance your feelings of optimism and hope about your loved one with an acceptance of reality about his situation. When thoughts about your loved one's dying appear, it is normal to feel a mixture of sorrow and relief.

► Experiencing these feelings can be beneficial. Those who care for loved ones through long illnesses have been reported to have fewer negative health effects after the death than those whose loved ones died suddenly or quickly. You have the opportunity to work through these feelings and come to resolution and peace with them.

―⸻⸻―

My expectations of myself were so high when my mother became ill with cancer. I thought I had to be the perfect caregiver daughter. My own life is filled with a job, two teenage sons, and a husband who travels for his work. I realized I was feeling resentful about having to drive and see Mother every day in the nursing facility. Then I felt guilty for having those feelings.

After doing a little reading—and a lot of reflection—I realized I needed to accept and forgive myself for some of these feelings. I know I can't give over my entire life to caregiving; I need to do things for me. Forgiving both myself and her has helped me get over my negative thoughts about myself. Now I say to myself, "No more guilt," and it is so healing.

Maureen, 50

Backup Care Plans

One of the best things you can do to prevent and relieve stress related to caregiving is to have a very good backup care plan. This is a plan that is called into service when you are not available or when you need a break from caregiving.

A great worry may be what would happen if you are not able to be there when your loved one needs you. Preparing a backup care plan is best done when things are going well.

Start by reviewing the types of ongoing care that your loved one needs everyday. Make a list of those needs. Is it help getting up in the morning or going to bed at night? Is it assistance with meals? Is it someone to be available if the professional caregiver doesn't show up? Or does your loved one need full-time supervision because of serious physical or mental limitations?

Consider who might provide backup for each of those needs. When Robert's mother was just home from rehabilitation, she had 24-hour home health care. Then they decided she would be safe alone at night. They had an emergency call button service, but because Robert traveled a great deal for his job, he really felt she needed to have someone close by who could be *on call* during the night. Robert hired a woman whom he paid a small monthly fee, plus an hourly fee if she were called to be with his mother.

Divide up the caregiving so that you are more comfortable asking people to help. Some things can be done by friends, neighbors, members of your parents' faith community, a volunteer from a community group, or a teenager whom you hire. By having several people available to step in, you'll find that if one person is sick or unavailable, the entire backup plan doesn't fall apart.

When Barbara's father was disabled by a stroke, Barbara created a list of five friends who would be willing to provide assistance if one of the professional caregivers did not show up. Barbara's mother was living at home with her father, but she was not able to provide the physical care he needed. She had the list of names and numbers posted next to the telephone. As it turned out, she never needed to call any of Barbara's friends, but it gave them both great peace of mind.

Having a backup care plan can relieve stress and anxiety, knowing that there will be immediate assistance for your loved one. It can also be as source of support when you, yourself, need respite from caregiving.

Elizabeth, my wife of 25 years, was just diagnosed with breast cancer. Neither of us was prepared for all that would be required for her treatment—doctors' appointments, radiation, chemotherapy. I'm a plumber, so I have flexibility with my work schedule and have been able to be with her at most appointments. But there is the occasional work emergency, so I knew we needed to have a backup plan.

Elizabeth and I made up a list of people who were available during the day in case I couldn't take her to an appointment. Because Elizabeth often feels miserable after a treatment, we also made a list of family and close friends who could come over if I was called away in the middle of the night to fix someone's leaky pipe. It's a comfort to me knowing she will not be alone while I'm gone. We have not had to use many of these folks but having them on call puts my mind at ease.

Sam, 67

Mixed Emotions

Life's changes and transition points are frequently times of mixed, and often conflicting, emotions. The start of a new chapter always means the ending of some other chapter. No one knows this better than parents and caregivers of aging relatives. When adult children leave home or get married, parents often experience mixed emotions. They are likely to feel excited that their adult child is moving forward with his own life and, at the same time, nostalgic about when he was a young child.

Caregivers regularly experience closing and opening chapters—transition points; caregiving is rarely the same for very long. The transitions can be abrupt or gradual. When Ralph's mother had a massive stroke, the event created a dramatic transition point for her and for the whole family. As his father aged, the closing and opening of chapters were less obvious and sometimes only recognizable in hindsight, like his father's stopping driving, needing support with housecleaning, needing help with pills, needing assistance with money management. When one chapter closes and your loved one moves into a new chapter, you let go of some things, too. These may include the way you view your loved one or how you interact with him or her. There is an adjustment period in this, sometimes so brief as to be unnoticeable. In addition, the many demands in life may force you to shift your role with your loved one without ever giving you a chance to acknowledge and honor the feelings that accompany these adjustments.

When Ralph finally had to place his father in a long-term care facility, he immediately felt very guilty; he felt as though he had failed his father. At the same time, he felt relief. The constant worry about his father's safety was lifted. Ralph felt a kind of freedom. He was also secretly excited that he would have more time to spend with his children and on other interests.

Mixed emotions, even conflicting emotions, are a normal component of change. When you find yourself at the next transition point with your loved one, take a deep breath and acknowledge your mixed emotions. Let yourself experience the whole array of feelings. As you allow the feelings to be felt, they will lessen and align as a chapter is closed and another opens.

———

When Ken was diagnosed with advanced cancer, I went through every emotion in the book. I was so scared for him and wondered how much longer he would live. At the same time, I was afraid for myself for two reasons: I had been a caregiver for my father during many of my younger years, and I knew how hard a job it was. I dreaded the prospect of caring for my husband. I was also afraid for myself, that I would soon be alone. Ken and I married young, so I had never been alone. I didn't want Ken to die, for his sake but also for mine. That felt pretty selfish, to be thinking of myself at a time like this. But I let those feelings come out and even began to make plans about how and where I would live if Ken died. It may have seemed morbid to someone else, but it seemed right to me. I felt better having acknowledged and experienced those feelings.

Jill, 75

Flipping the Stress Switch

Stop the world, I want to get off! As a caregiver, you probably know the feeling.

You can't stop the world, but you can stop yourself when things move too fast. You can stop what you're doing and consider, for a moment, what you are trying to accomplish. Is there a balance among your activities or are you trying to do everything yourself? Is there something you could accomplish more easily if you asked for help? Could you pace yourself and still get things done without feeling like you're running around in circles?

When you're juggling a busy schedule, it is easy to feel scattered. When you're feeling scattered, your thinking may not be productive, so when it happens, stop and pull your energy back. Here's a simple and brief exercise to help you do that.

► Sit down, close your eyes, and take a deep breath or two. Then, focus on your own breathing.

► Feel the energy in and around your body. This might feel like tingling or perhaps warmth.

► Next, draw all the energy back into yourself. Maybe you imagine it gathering around your heart.

► Continue to sit quietly with your eyes closed for a few more moments. Play with the idea of having a mental *off* switch, one that lets you go inside yourself for some peace and quiet. It is especially important if you don't have much time alone. Even a ten-minute break can be very refreshing, if you can stop all activity and become still. You don't have to go through every minute of every day being switched *on.*

► To flip the *off* switch remember to *stop and reflect* (ask yourself if what you're trying to do is balanced), *stop and be alone* (close your eyes and focus on your breathing), and *stop and be still* (mentally retrieve your scattered energy).

When you switch back *on*, you'll be more relaxed and able to handle your caregiving responsibilities with greater clarity and focus.

———

Living with someone with Alzheimer's disease grows more stressful each day. Because the condition gradually reduced my wife's mental capabilities, I suppose I had just acclimated to each stage. It wasn't until I found myself losing my patience with her that I recognized the stress I was under. It wasn't good for my wife and certainly not good for me. So now, while my wife watches her favorite television program, I step out on the patio for a few quiet minutes. I inhale the aroma of the garden. It has been a pleasure to feel revived and relaxed after even a short break.

Jackson, 70

CHAPTER THREE

Circle 2: **The Caregiver's Relationship with the Care Recipient**

T HE NEXT CIRCLE OUT FROM THE CENTER considers the caregiver's relationship with the care receiver. This is the key relationship when caregiving and one that is often fraught with challenges. Typically the caregiver–care receiver relationship is in a state of flux because of the changing condition of the care receiver. Some caregivers may find themselves grieving the impending loss of their loved one. They may also find themselves so caught up in the busyness of caregiving that they feel they don't have time to step back and think about or attend to this relationship.

In this section I encourage you to step back from the day to day and get the "big picture" view of your relationship with the person for whom you are caring. This is an opportunity to heal past hurts and say goodbye. I hope you are inspired by the articles and the stories in this circle to create a relationship with the person for whom you are caring that will allow you to look back on your caregiving experience with peacefulness, completion, and no major regrets.

Rekindling Your True Role

Melanie is the primary caregiver for her 90-year-old mother. She related some wisdom she had learned from her neighbor whose son has autism. Melanie's neighbor said that over the years, she had spent countless hours arranging for services for her son, consulting with teachers and therapists, teaching him new skills, and driving him to appointments. In her attempt to help him reach his full potential, she became her son's therapist and teacher and chauffeur, and she forgot her true role, her son's mother. So, she began spending more time enjoying him and loving him and nurturing him.

Caregivers, too, take on many roles in their attempts to help their loved ones maintain the highest quality of life possible. Melanie recognized the pattern in herself; she had become just about everything to her mother. She took her mother to doctors' appointments, arranged for home care, and installed safety devices in the house to make it safer. All of these were important, to be sure. But Melanie began to feel like an unpaid social worker rather than a daughter. That is when she took the time to step back, to remember her true role, and to find ways to enjoy her mother again. Here are some ideas to help you regain perspective.

► Set some time aside—even 15 minutes—to sit and talk with your loved one. If she has dementia, she may not be able to converse with you as she used to, but *you* can still talk. Talk about things that give both of you pleasure, rather than focusing on issues related to care needs.

► Find an activity that you can do together and enjoy. Time pressures may cause you to spend time with him only when it is task related. Creating time to have fun together can be one of the best ways to rekindle the true relationship.

► Reminisce together, recall good memories. Tell stories that remind you of your true connection. You can encourage each other to remember stories about things that have brought you both joy.

► Laugh, again and again and again. Caregiving can be such serious business that it is easy to forget to laugh. If you can't find things to laugh about in your day-to-day activities, rent a funny movie that you can watch together. Laughing together can make you feel connected.

Reestablishing your true role can make the caregiving experience more joyful for you both. Creativity and a spirit of playfulness will help you in discovering ways to rebalance your relationship. It takes very little effort, and the payoff can be enormous.

⚊⚊

My father was doing so well after Mother's death until he fell on the stairs. It seemed like that was the end of his independence. Because my job does not have structured hours, Dad seemed to assume I could come whenever he needed me. I was running out two and three times a day doing errands and taking him to doctors, physical therapy, out for meals, and the like. I began to think of myself more as his servant than his daughter.

One day when I realized how angry I'd become, I said, "Dad, I love you, and we have got to get some help so I can be your daughter again." I think it hit him at that moment what he had been expecting of me. He put his arms around me and said, "You're right, I need to take care of my little girl."

Now I help him when I am with him and am very glad to do it. Hiring a companion to help with the appointments and errands has helped us reestablish our father-daughter relationship.

I would tell anyone who is caring for someone who is ill or disabled, not to take it "all" on. Preserve your relationship with the person you love.

Laura, 42

Be Here Now

One of the greatest gifts you can give your loved one is simply being present with him or her. Don't feel you always have to fix, cure, advise, treat, or rescue.

Your mere presence shows your willingness to bear witness to the experience, without pushing or pulling him or her along to a different state of being. When your loved one is feeling down or sad, you can just be with him in his feeling instead of becoming a cheerleader, attempting to make him (and perhaps you) feel better.

Here are five ideas on how to simply be there for your loved one and offer him or her the gift of your total presence.

► Pay close attention to your loved one. Stop whatever you are doing, and focus just on her. Think of it as turning a spotlight on and shining it fully on her.

► Try to be present, without an agenda. Don't simply comfort or reassure, trying to move your loved one out of his feelings. He may wind up with a feeling of isolation in the very midst of his loving family.

► The intent is not to keep your loved one happy but rather to keep her company, to help her hear herself more clearly. Think of how good you feel when a close friend allows you to say anything, and you know you will not be judged or rescued or even agreed with— just heard.

► It is often helpful to ask a question that will allow your loved one to explore what he is feeling and to get to the truth in the experience. Use words like *what* and *how* rather than *why*, which could make him feel defensive. Try things like: "What are those tears about?" "What bothers you the most?" "What's the hardest thing about this?" "What does that mean to you?"

► Follow your loved one's lead. If she says something, ask a *what* or *how* question about what she has said. Use active listening phrases like "seems like you are feeling" or "tell me about that."

Your loved one will feel respected and honored by your willingness to listen to him or her. Then you won't have to feel responsible for making the situation better or cheering him or her up. This approach of simply being present and listening will often improve the situation.

—⬤⬤—

Mother is slowly slipping away. I thought if I were doing something all the time I could stop the slide. A very kind friend at work heard about what was going on with my mother, and he saw how frazzled I'd become. We went to lunch at a quiet outdoor café, and he suggested I try a few things that had worked for him. They all centered around simply tuning into Mother and tuning out everything else.

Now I sit quietly with Mother in her room. Sometimes, she will say things, and I listen and ask her questions. We have had a few conversations, not very long ones, but I think she felt connected to me. I know I feel more useful now than I ever did when I was scurrying around doing things. Loving her and listening mean the most now.

Randy, 42

Reach Out and Touch Someone

As you get caught up in the daily tasks and activities of caregiving, you might find it difficult to maintain a sense of affection for your loved one. And yet, it is at just this time when both caregiver and patient need that affection most.

If you've ever parented or been around a teenager, you probably remember how he or she withdrew at even the slightest sign of affection. This is a natural part of the drive for independence. Most parents, though, don't give up; we grab the occasional hug or a brief caress in order to maintain that connection. On some level, we know that effort was appreciated.

So, it is equally important to stay connected with your loved one through touch. We know that human touch—hand holding, hugs, back rubs, and simple direct eye contact—can have a powerful calming effect. Further, being touched by a loved one is even more calming than being touched by a stranger. We also know that babies who are not held and cuddled can fail to thrive. Likewise, if we lack affection and touch, we become sad and upset.

How can you maintain or reestablish that physical contact with your loved one in a meaningful way? Here are some thoughts.

➤ In what new ways could you show affection, even if it is one-sided? You might rub pleasant-smelling lotion on your loved one's dry skin. Or massage his tender bald head—a result of chemotherapy. Could you gently move her stiff joint? You both, then, have the benefit of touch and its calming effect.

➤ If you are caring for a spouse or partner, your previous sex life may be only a memory. To what extent can you still be intimate; what would the medical condition allow? It might be that holding hands is enough, or snuggling together on the couch or in bed. Perhaps adding a romantic atmosphere with dimmed lights and candles can enhance intimacy. The brain has been called the most important sex organ!

► Say, "I love you," as often as possible. That feeling of love may have changed since your loved one became ill. You could feel like the long-term chronically ill person is less lovable, that he's taking more love than he's giving. Try, then, to identify things about him that are lovable and mention them regularly.

Reach out and touch your loved one. It will make both of you feel so good, and it doesn't cost a cent.

It was so sad for me to watch Sidney decline so rapidly with Alzheimer's disease. We rarely shared a hug as he began his decline. Sid is not easy to love sometimes. But ever the romantic optimist, I decided to say, "I love you," every chance I had. Now I hold Sid's hand when we sit on the couch, and sometimes, I think a spark comes back for him. And that makes it light for me, too. I feel so much better about myself, and once I started, it became a natural way to make contact with Sid, who is still there with me.

Rachel, 68

Give Illness the Attention It Needs but No More

It may feel like the illness of your loved one has consumed your life, and, in many ways, it has. At the same time, it is important to keep the illness, and its impact on your life, in perspective. The illness does not define your loved one or his or her life. The trick, then, is to focus on helping him or her live life to the fullest.

You can help your loved one keep this perspective on the illness. One simple way is to encourage him to maintain, to the extent possible, his normal routines—checking the weather forecast, reading the financial pages, following his investments, or working in the garden.

A caregiver named Mike went to great efforts to keep his wife from focusing all her energies on her heart disease. He reminded her that she was *not* the disease. Rather, it is a part of who she is and, indeed, a part of her life, but it does not define her *whole* life. In the same way, Mike reminded his wife that they never thought of their friend Ted, who lost his arm in an accident, as a handicapped person, rather that Ted's a person who happens to have a handicap.

Let's face it, this illness does take up lots of space in your life and your loved one's life. It affects daily routines and activities. It takes time and energy to get to doctors and treatment appointments and to cope with pain and discomfort. The key to balance is to give the illness the attention it needs but no more. Make room for it, but try not to let it take over.

Sheila's father had become totally focused on his cancer and finding ways to prolong his life. He was not using the time he had to enjoy the life he was trying to prolong. Sheila tried to remind him that they should figure out ways to enjoy the time they had together rather than using that time to worry about the future. If the treatment succeeded in providing more time, then they needed to make sure they maximized that extra time, too.

⬥

My husband, Mark, has severe heart disease. He used to be very active, the leader of any group he was in. When he found out he had limitations, it made him want to stop everything he loved altogether. We never realized we had let his condition become a third party in our home.

In a fit of mutual frustration, we decided that while we cannot deny Mark's illness, and the time and energy

*it takes, we would not allow it to become our only
focus. Now we focus on what he can do, not what he
can't. His heart disease no longer dominates our life. Of
course, we do not pretend he has no limitations, but it is
so refreshing to feel that Mark and I are in control—not
the illness.*

Zora, 67

He Never Says Thank You

Many caregivers, perhaps including you, have loved ones who
are not easy to care for or are unpleasant or seem ungrateful.
Caring for someone who expresses little or no appreciation
adds a layer of stress to an already stressful role. It can certainly
make it harder to experience the positive aspects of caregiving.

What can you do if this is your situation? How you can
maximize the positive aspects of caregiving, and there are
many, despite your loved one's apparent lack of gratitude?
Here are some things to think about.

► Choose how you want to behave as a caregiver—completely separate from the reaction of your loved one.
Think about the reason you are a caregiver in the first
place. It's probably not for the praise. More than likely
you do it because you want the best for your loved one.

It is hard not to react to someone's negative behavior. Yet, the only behavior you can control is your own.
You may find that you have to remind yourself, over and
over, of your reason for giving this loving care when
your loved one is grouchy or seems unappreciative.

► Ask yourself what you can learn from your loved one's
behavior. What can you learn about who you want to be
in the world, how you want to treat others, and how you
want to act as you, yourself, age? Many caregivers find

they are more positive, grateful people because of the experience of caregiving for a difficult person. This is truly making the most of a challenging situation!

► If possible, and appropriate, talk to your loved one about how his or her behavior makes you feel. It is true that we teach people how to treat us, so we don't have to settle for unpleasant behavior. If you choose to talk to your loved one, strive to be able to express your feelings in a respectful and kind manner; don't try to change his or her behavior. Rather, express your feelings about how he or she is treating you.

► We all need acknowledgment. This is where your friends can be helpful. Call someone you can vent to and who can remind you what a wonderful job you are doing. This type of contact can help you through rough patches with more grace and ease.

———

My sister and I have always had a prickly relationship. When Sally was diagnosed with cancer, it was pretty far along. I knew she would need my help. I moved to her home while she was in treatment. She was in discomfort and, sometimes, pain so I was very patient and loving with her. As she improved, it seemed as though she became less sensitive to what she said to me. It felt like I could never do anything to satisfy her. I realized she never really thanked me for anything I did. One day when I had prepared her favorite dinner, she finished and left the room. I did some thinking that night and decided I want to be here for her but I need to talk to her about how I feel when she doesn't value my help.

The next day we talked. She was quite surprised when I told her some of my feelings. She said she would

try to be more considerate, and I hugged her and told
her that it made me feel better just knowing she cared
about how I felt.

Sometimes her behavior still upsets me, and when
it does, I talk with my husband and let out some of my
hurt. He's wonderfully supportive and knows I love my
sister and want the best for her.

Muriel, 69

Sometimes I Feel So Dishonest

Perhaps one of the most difficult issues in caring for a sick loved one is that we, from time to time, need to say or do things that may not be totally honest. It's all part of realizing that you no longer have the same relationship that you did before your loved one became ill.

There are two components to the changes you may experience when a loved one loses mental capacity. Your loved one no longer has the ability to converse on the variety of topics he or she used to and you may find you have to withhold some information from the very person with whom you've always shared everything.

The conversation changed for Brian and his father, both history buffs, when Dad developed dementia. They'd always loved to discuss famous wars with names of generals, dates of battles, and other historical details. As the dementia progressed, Brian stopped bringing up some of their favorite topics because his father became frustrated when he could not remember historical facts, and then he would become angry. Brian's solution was to find easy-to-understand books on military history at the library and read them to his Dad.

It can be even more devastating when you find you must hold back or alter the way you present information to your loved one. Joan agonizes over the fact that she can no longer talk about everything with her husband, who suffers from Alzheimer's disease. Joan and her husband had built a solid trust over their years of marriage and cherished the ability to be open and honest with each other. But as his mental capacity diminished, she could no longer talk with him about even household issues.

Before he became ill, Joan's husband handled their financial investing, and she served as a sounding board for his suggestions. Now that her husband is no longer able to make sound financial decisions, Joan is faced with a double burden. She must learn much more about their investments, and she must keep him from taking any actions that could negatively impact their financial situation. Joan has begun working with a financial planner and learning what she needs to know to manage their accounts. At the same time, she encourages her husband by regularly telling him what a great job he has done through the years with their investments and how all his hard work will now enable them to live in good financial shape.

Your relationships will, indeed, change when there is illness, especially loss of mental capacity. Don't think it dishonest to have to talk to loved ones in new ways. Rather, it is a loving attempt to create new ways of relating when the old ways no longer work.

In my parents' life together, Mom took care of domestic chores, and Dad was in charge of everything else. When Dad was diagnosed with Alzheimer's disease, Mom and I thought we would be able to help him enough that he could maintain a reasonably normal life. That idea evaporated when I looked over some financial reports.

I knew Mom and I would have to talk to the lawyer, accountant, and stockbroker to let them know

Dad was no longer able to think clearly, and we needed to establish safeguards to prevent his making terrible and costly errors. To make these contacts without telling Dad really felt disloyal. However, all the professionals told me that their interactions with Dad over the past year had been difficult for them. They were happy to work with me to avoid bad legal or financial actions.

It became necessary to take the next step and tell Dad he wasn't able to be in sole charge of decisions. We said that Mom and I would need to be informed about any financial or legal changes he thought about. Dad seemed upset for a short time and then he forgot. We now have all the legal paperwork in place and any change must be approved by Mom and me.

Mary Ann, 53

Seeing Your Loved One through New Eyes

Relationships with our loved ones can literally be transformed when we honor them as individuals—separate from us. One way is to see him or her as a stranger, someone you've just met. To paraphrase Marcel Proust, real discovery is not seeking new landscapes but having new eyes.

Try this for 24 hours. Listen to your loved one as though you have just met her, as though you knew nothing about her before this conversation. Just pretend that you are a stranger who doesn't have any history with her.

This technique can be successful if you want to re-create a long-term relationship. In these relationships there are always expectations of how the other person will react or respond. Before he even speaks, you are certain of what he will say. Or, if he starts to tell you a story you've heard before, you tune out. We often listen least to the people we love the most.

Beth tried this technique with her elderly father, who frequently tells her stories she's heard repeatedly through her life. She decided to listen to the stories as if they were being told by a stranger, someone she'd just met. Beth was pleasantly surprised by the results. She heard many things about her father's experiences during World War II in Panama that she'd never heard before—or at least never listened to before. Beth found herself genuinely interested in his stories, rather than just waiting for him to finish.

Because Beth was behaving as though she hadn't heard the stories countless times, she asked many questions. Her father was delighted and shared more stories with her. That day Beth learned things about her father she had never known. He felt valued and appreciated—two things we all want the most from the people we love.

This technique takes some practice. You don't have to do it perfectly to reap benefits, just remind yourself to try again when you slip back into your old ways. And, as you see your loved one through new eyes, imagine the new landscapes you discover.

———————

I didn't think I could listen to Mother for one more minute as a child. When I was in my twenties, I became an expert at blocking her out, which I did successfully until two years ago. It was then that she was incapacitated with a chronic lung disease.

I began to visit her more frequently, always dreading her constant chatter. After two months of this I was at my wit's end. My wife, in her wisdom, simply said, "Why don't you just listen more closely than you ever have before?" Indeed, why not try it? So I did. I decided to visit with the intention of hearing every word

Mother said as though I'd never heard it before. She quickly sensed my new-found interest, and we began to talk about things we'd never discussed before. I learned so much about my father and their life together, things I would never have known.

I take this approach with other family members and with difficult coworkers, as well. The results are remarkable for me, and it's such an easy thing to do.

Ron, 60

Put It into Words

Letting your loved one know now how much you care about him or her can benefit you as well. During these days filled with caregiving tasks, changing attitudes, and mood swings from your loved one, it's easy to begin to feel negative and even forget that you ever felt good.

One way to renew those good feelings is by allowing yourself to fill up with memories of the life you've shared with your loved one. In the glow of those memories, begin a conversation. You might record your thoughts and feelings and then play the recording for your loved one. You may have other family members and friends talk about their relationships with your loved one. With a little preparation, children can be particularly effective in talking about their memories and why your loved one is so special. A grandchild, for example, might remember the time Grandpa took him fishing.

Marisa started her conversation with the words "I just want you to know how grateful I am for all that you have meant to me." She and her sister made a recording for their mother in which they reminisced about the many gifts their mother had given them, like the fun of giving a party or the ability to find a good bargain.

When you talk, include the sad stories along with the good. One way to reaffirm your relationship bond is to talk about difficult times you have weathered together. Leo initiates conversations with his ailing wife by mentioning a few bad stock market investments they have made. They enjoy dreaming about how they would have spent the money they'd expected to make and usually wind up laughing about their lack of skill in predicting what the market would do.

Sharing conversations about a past family tragedy can bring you closer together now. It may create a sense of empowerment that you will both be able to get through the current situation because you have made it through difficult times before.

Whether you make a recording or talk directly with your loved one, the important thing is to reestablish or strengthen the bond that may have worn a bit thin in the new relationship as caregiver and patient. Such conversations can help you remember just how much your loved one means to you and renew your efforts to provide a loving environment for him or her.

—⁓⊶⁓—

I had become so emotionally disconnected from my mother as she declined with Parkinson's and emphysema. All I could think about was everything I had to do—every day, every week.

One day in the fall, as the leaves fell, I realized just how little time we had left to talk to each other. I cried and then resolved to find some time at least two or three times a week to just sit and talk with Mom. I went into her storage area and brought out some wonderful old pictures. We had a great time poring over these together. Over the last month, the richness of our relationship has returned. We laugh at old memories

and sigh when we look at some of the old pictures. I've
encouraged my brother in Colorado to come soon and
just visit with Mom while she can still enjoy his com-
pany. Some of my tasks don't get done now, but that
doesn't matter. I will never regret taking that time with
my mother.

Sylvia, 60

Sharing and Creating Memories

For caregivers, it is easy to get consumed by all of the tasks, appointments, and phone calls that you have to handle. When that happens, it's easy to lose sight of one of the best parts of caregiving: sharing laughter with your loved one.

Laughter makes us feel more alive and connected with each other. It lowers our stress level and increases our feelings of well-being. We both—caregiver and care receiver—can use a little laughter in our lives. Sometimes, though, things just don't seem funny, or you are just plain out of ideas on how to lighten up the situation. Here are some ways that might help you enjoy your time with your ill loved one.

Spend time together recalling funny memories you have shared as a family. You might want to think of a few stories ahead of time to get the conversation started. It is likely that as you tell one or two funny memories, you will trigger your loved one's memory of others. This is a wonderful way to spend time together, reminiscing and laughing.

Todd asked his grandmother to tell him about her childhood. He realized that when he was a child, he would tune Grandma out whenever she started talking about the old days. Now he'd remind her of a story she'd told and then ask her to fill in the details. His grandmother was pleased at his interest and happily recounted incidents from her life. Todd developed a great respect for his grandmother as he learned the many impressive things she had accomplished.

You might rent funny movies. This is a wonderful way to spend a couple of hours laughing together. Look for movies from your loved one's youth; they may trigger memories of when he or she first saw these films. Also look for DVDs of comedians that he or she might enjoy.

Pull out the old photo albums. This time, as you look through the pictures, spend time recalling as much as you can about what was happening in both of your lives at the time the picture was taken. Don't forget to focus on some of the changing hair and clothing styles, which are always good for some laughs!

Sometimes when we are caregiving our natural tendency is to look backward rather than forward, especially with an aging relative. One of the best things about joyfully recalling memories is that you will also be making new memories together.

—◦◦◦◦—

Elaine, my wife, had become almost totally silent as she slowly crept deeper into Alzheimer's. My daughter mentioned something she had heard about the value of touching old memories and suggested Elaine and I might enjoy watching some of the old movies we had enjoyed together. She helped me locate many of them, and her husband got us set up to see them on DVD. To hear Elaine laugh, even a little, was the best sound I had heard in two years. We held hands when we watched love stories.

I truly believe this stimulation has kept Elaine with me for several extra months.

Why didn't I think of such a simple idea? I guess because I was focusing on Elaine's death, and not her

*life. When you are a caregiver it is so easy to lose sight
of the person, and only focus on the patient. Now, I'll
have gentle memories because I found Elaine again.*

Ernie, 78

What Is Unfinished?

In the midst of the myriad activities of caregiving, it is easy to
forget that you will not always have your loved one with you.
From time to time you may need to remember to step back
and have a look at the larger caregiving perspective and at the
loved one for whom you are providing care. A way to shift the
perspective is to ask what is unfinished in your relationship
with your loved one or what might you regret not having said.

It is often painful to look toward the time when your loved
one is gone, yet doing so can prevent emotional pain in the
future. If you can ask yourself these tough questions now, they
won't nag you later. Here are other thoughts that might help
you shift the perspective.

- ► What would you like to say thank you for?

- ► Are there things for which you'd like to say, I'm sorry or
  I forgive you?

- ► Is there anything you need to ask for? An explanation, an
  apology?

- ► Are there things you said or did that you would like to
  explain?

- ► Are there special memories you'd like to talk about?

- ► Is there a relative only your loved one remembers and
  whom you'd like to know about?

What if your loved one has dementia and can't respond
or may not understand what you are saying? There may be

questions that you would like to ask that you now can't. However, if you have something to say, say it anyway! Unless what you are sharing is going to cause someone pain, go ahead and share it.

Casey learned his mother was dying only a month before she passed away. He had a day with her during which he got to say the things he needed and wanted to say to her. Because of a stroke nearly eight years before, his mother was unable to respond. Casey wasn't sure how much she was able to understand, but he spoke from his heart and has never regretted that he did.

So, ask yourself what is unfinished in the relationship. Ask yourself what you might wish you'd said when you had the chance. Then listen to your heart; it will give you the right answers.

—◁▥◁◊▥▷—

My husband and I had drifted apart. After 43 years of marriage, we rarely talked about anything that mattered. One day on the way to work, he was in a terrible automobile accident. What followed was a difficult time in the hospital and then at home.

At first, we only talked about the problems, the doctors, the treatment. Time passed, but he did not improve. It became quickly apparent that I would lose George. My feelings of regret were so strong that they moved me to consider what I wanted him to know before he left me. That opened the floodgates—memories, thoughts, gratitude poured in.

I told George I really needed to talk to him, and he wanted to listen. Sometimes he was under heavy medication, but we spent time each day, holding hands, remembering good times and bad. I asked for his forgiveness for my turning away when he needed me. We both agreed that we had so much to be thankful for. We spoke of love, we laughed, and we talked about my future.

When George died I grieved terribly but not for what we hadn't said. Our second chance came and we took it by sharing all we could fit in. I don't feel we left anything unfinished, and for that I am grateful.

Lynette, 68

CHAPTER FOUR

Circle 3: **Relationships with Family and Close Friends**

THE NEXT CONCENTRIC CIRCLE considers our relationships with family and friends. At their best, these relationships sustain and nurture us and reduce the burdens of caregiving. At their worst, these relationships drain our energy and add to our burdens. Many caregivers are somewhere between these two extremes: they have some family and friends who are supportive and others who add to their stress.

In this section you will find many ideas for maximizing the support you get from your family and friends and reducing any disharmony that might exist in these relationships. The importance of this should not be underestimated. Research studies consistently confirm that healthy and supportive relationships actually keep us healthy—both physically and mentally. These relationships also can be key for sharing the many tasks of caregiving.

Keeping Others Informed

Caregivers can become exhausted just trying to keep everyone updated on the changing health condition of a loved one. This is especially true if there is chronic illness or crisis.

Family and friends will often check to see how your loved

one is doing and how you are managing. You may find yourself telling the same stories over and over again. The conversation may end with, "Please call me and let me know how things are going. I'm concerned about you." Even though their intention is to be loving and supportive, you may feel as though having to contact all of these people only adds to your work.

That is exactly how Nellie felt. She said that any time she wasn't with her mother at the hospital she was on the phone updating people on her mother's condition. She couldn't get a break. Nellie knew she had to have some help with this. How could she keep people informed and not feel depleted herself? Being a generally organized person, Nellie came up with her own ideas. See if they'll work for you.

► Set up a telephone tree. You would then call only one person, who would call one or two others, who in turn would call others, until everyone gets the news. You may set up several telephone trees—family, friends, work colleagues, church friends. Then when there is news you call one designated person for each group. This alone may be the difference between being over-whelmed or not.

► Send a group email instead of calling people. This allows you to send one message and be done.

► Tell anyone who wants to be informed that you will contact them when there is a change in the situation. If there is no change you will contact them every so many days (you pick how often).

► You may need to be direct but gentle with people who continue to call you despite your having set up a system. Let them know you appreciate the concern but that it is difficult for you, amid all your tasks and duties, to speak with everyone directly. Telling the same story over and over is exhausting, and you may have to let those frequent callers know. Perhaps that frequent caller could be #1 on your telephone tree.

► Determine what will make you feel supported by people. A card? An email or voice mail message? Someone to bring dinner? Whatever it is, communicate it clearly so that the people who love you can support you in ways that are meaningful to you.

The more open and honest you can be about your needs, the more likely people are to respond to them. Often we act as though people are mind readers and then are surprised and hurt when they don't behave as we would hope.

You can keep people informed but also set boundaries that allow you to take a break from caregiving. You may need to be creative and persistent, but it will definitely be worth your time.

━━━◦◦━━━

I am the caregiver for my 40-year-old daughter, Carol, who has multiple sclerosis. People are very kind and solicitous about my situation. Not only do my friends want information but Carol's friends also want contact with me.

Carol's cousin, and best friend, Janie suggested that I set up an email list of Carol's friends. That way, I could send our updates easily. Janie helped me create the mailing list and showed me just what to do. Carol has been so pleased to get responses from her friends.

We still speak directly with family and a few close friends. It's given me a real energy boost knowing how and what information is distributed. Now, when I run into someone in a store who asks me, "How's Carol?" I keep it simple and don't feel bad about doing it.

Beth, 65

Playing to Our Family Members' Strengths

Natalie's husband's health had been declining for several years. A friend asked how Ted, Natalie's adult son and only child, was doing with all the changes. Natalie said Ted came home every other weekend and was extremely helpful with many of the tasks that needed to be done.

Natalie had the wisdom and awareness to see that this was Ted's way of being a support to both her and his father. She said that it was not Ted's nature to sit and talk to her about the situation—she had friends to fill that role. He showed his love and support in the ways that he could, which included being there and helping out with tasks.

This story points out just how much easier and more harmonious caregiving could be if we appreciated, as graciously as Natalie did, the ways in which our family members contribute and allowed them to play to their strengths.

In order to do that, you need to have a large enough *support squad* so you aren't relying on one or two people to do everything. Here are some ideas for developing your own support squad.

Make a list of the people you can call, email, or get together with for support. Note their contact information and their positions on your squad. For example, some people are great when you feel in crisis—they can "talk you off the ledge." Other upbeat friends may help shift your view by sharing a laugh, while someone else might be a research expert, serving as your human encyclopedia on specific medical information. Always keep the list handy and update it as you make new connections.

Then, ask yourself who is missing from your support squad. What frustrates you because it isn't getting done or done the way you'd like? What do you wish family members were doing to help with the caregiving; what do you find yourself complaining about? Once you've identified what's missing, you can find people who are willing and able to do it. Don't hesitate to ask others for help finding these squad members. Always be ready to tap into the strengths of others.

I have to admit being frustrated with my niece and nephew, who just did not want to spend time with their grandfather although his health was declining fast. I decided to sit them down and talk about the situation. What I learned was they had never been around someone so sick before and had never seen a person who had died.

They told me that they felt terrible about not visiting Grandpa more often, but they were just plain scared to be with him, in case something happened while they were there. Then, we talked about ways that they could be helpful, and they were glad to take on jobs like yard work and shopping. We arranged to have them visit Grandpa only when I or another adult was present, so they would not be afraid.

Our conversation turned the whole situation around so I got extra help from them in ways that felt comfortable to them and they were grateful to be playing a role in caring for the grandfather they loved.

Gertrude, 62

We Need Our Friends

While caregiving may sometimes feel like the most solitary journey, in truth, friends play an important supporting role. There are many different ways that our friends can and want to support us. So consider accepting the offer of help.

A couple of Virginia's closest friends pulled together a local network of friends to help when her husband's illness limited what he could do. The friends provided what Virginia needed during each phase of the caregiving experience. When her husband's illness was first diagnosed, the network of friends provided transportation to doctor visits and tests and fixed meals for Virginia and her husband when they arrived home from the appointments. The friends arranged regular visits with her husband so Virginia could get out for a few hours.

As the illness progressed and her husband became housebound, Virginia needed to hire professional help to care for him. The friends continued to visit but for shorter periods. These visits provided her husband with some stimulation during the day and gave Virginia a chance for a quick chat with her friend. The friends network arranged to run local errands, and one talented gardener friend would do a little weeding and pruning when she visited.

Distant friends can also be a great source of comfort. Ann was touched when she received a package from a group of close friends from New York. The six friends had met in a class when Ann was living in New York, and they continued to meet for many years. Her friends created a beautiful package filled with fun gifts for Ann; it included funny movies, a TV comedy series, an inspirational book, and a wide range of music CDs. Along with the gifts, each friend included a personal note saying that friendship was forever and that they were thinking of and praying for Ann during this difficult time.

Of course, friends can stay connected through email communication. John prefers not to receive phone calls, especially during the evening when he spends time with his ill wife. He has asked friends to send emails, with the understanding that he will feel no pressure to respond. In fact, he sends a group email from time to time with an update on his wife's situation.

Within this message, he takes the opportunity to express gratitude for all the caring and support he has received.

Here is a thought John received in an email note from a friend, "When you have to walk that lonesome valley and you have to walk it by yourself, the friends in your life will be on the valley's rim, cheering you on, praying for you, pulling for you, intervening on your behalf, and waiting with open arms at the valley's end. Sometimes, they will even break the rules and walk beside you. Or come in and carry you out."

When we learned that Ralph's cancer had returned, I wanted to hide from everyone. I felt so down and depressed. But my friend Blanche wouldn't let me do that, and she formed a network of friends that has sustained us for the past four months. Friends are a must, I have learned. They can walk along with you and help to lift the burden.

Ralph was so relieved to see me get this support. I vowed never again to hide but rather to accept the offered hand of friendship.

Sally, 69

Creating Realistic Expectations

It is critical that caregivers and family of an ill loved one hold realistic expectations of caregiving. There are four factors that come into play when you are caring for your loved one, and they figure prominently into setting expectations for all involved.

▶ Proximity. Where do family caregivers live in relation to the care receiver? There are some things that can only be

done by someone living nearby and other things that
can be done no matter where the caregiver lives.

► Relationships. What are the relationships between the
family caregivers and the care receiver? A family member
with a strained relationship with the care recipient may
not be as receptive to caregiving tasks as one that has a
warm relationship with the care recipient.

► Life stage. What are the life stages of all the family caregivers? For example, does one family member have small
children while another's children are grown? Is one family member's career in a phase-out mode while another's
is still gearing up?

► Financial. What is the financial status of the family caregivers? It may not be reasonable to expect each family
member to contribute financially. Sometimes there is
one family caregiver who is able to contribute financially
when the others can not.

It is important to set realistic expectations when dividing
the caregiving tasks among family members. If you are the lead
caregiver, you could suggest an in-person or telephone family
meeting to discuss each of these factors and how they will
impact how you divide the caregiving tasks and responsibilities.
In such a meeting, each family member would be given the
opportunity to offer his or her perspective on the four factors.

These factors don't constitute a formula; they do not add
up to a single answer about how all of the caregiving tasks will
be accomplished. Instead what emerges is a picture that allows
everyone to understand everyone else's situation. That way,
you can have a more realistic discussion about who in the family can most easily do what. This provides a discussion tool
that can promote understanding and harmony.

Some families will not hold a family meeting under any

circumstances. If that is true for your family, you can still set realistic expectations for yourself and your family members if you are willing to take the time to consider these factors. Yes, you can do this exercise alone and still see benefits.

The more specific you can be about what you need help with, the more likely a family member will step in. Often family members don't help with caregiving because they don't know what needs to be done. You may think that your family members do, or should, know, but it is still better to make concrete requests. Family members may be more willing when the clear need is expressed.

⚊⚋⚊

I'd held the idea that my sister, brother, and I would all share the caregiving tasks for our mother. I was sadly mistaken. My sister lives 2000 miles away and has young children. My brother is closer, but he is uncomfortable facing the seriousness of Mother's illness. It became clear that I had to take charge and find a reasonable way to share the responsibility, which didn't mean dividing it up equally.

I looked at my siblings' strengths and weaknesses, and then thought about which one's lifestyle would best suit which task. Because of the distance, we couldn't come together as a family so we started with conference calls. These calls became very important to us, and I, as the primary caregiver, felt supported and encouraged in what I did. I never thought that we could do this until I really looked at my sister and brother and realized we each had something to give toward Mom's care. Our unified approach to our mother's care needs has helped her and made her feel proud of all of us.

Emily, 59

Decision Making: A Family Affair

Caregivers often struggle with feelings of guilt and regret when they must place a loved one in a nursing home or other care facility. They wonder if they should have tried harder to keep their loved one at home. Often, though, it is the best decision not only for the loved one but also for the family.

One of the hardest things about eldercare planning is that decisions we make for our aging family members affect the entire family. Desiree had tried to provide the best care possible for her father, who had Alzheimer's disease, while also responding to the needs of her older, frail mother. At the same time, she attended to her own family and held down a job. Desiree could feel her own burnout. This family had worked diligently to keep her father home as long as possible, utilizing a day care program for persons with Alzheimer's and employing professional caregivers in the home. Yet her father's disease continued to progress and he became aggressive toward his wife. Finally, his incontinence and violent moods were more than Desiree's frail mother could handle or the medications could control. Only then did Desiree place her father in a nursing home.

Often in an attempt to do the best for an aging family member, a caregiver endures schedules and levels of stress that are hard to imagine. But care decisions made for a loved one must take into account how they will impact the entire family—not just the patient. Decisions that appear to be good for an aging family member but terrible for one or more other family members can often be bad decisions. Family members may become resentful of losing their own quality of life to maintain the quality of life of their aging relative.

How can you balance the needs of everyone, including your own, when planning eldercare? One way is to list the names of the people who will be affected, and how, by a particular decision. You are not trying to make the perfect decision, only the best decision for a difficult situation. What if your aging relative expects the family to be at his beck and call? In truth, you may never be successful at getting him to consider the needs of others. Some aging relatives try to use guilt and shame as a way to force families into their preferred care situations, regardless of the family impact. Caregiving and eldercare planning are best considered a family affair, with all members accounted for as decisions and plans are made.

When Mom was diagnosed with Alzheimer's disease, she made us promise that we would never put her in a care facility, no matter how bad she got. Her own parents had bad nursing home experiences; the facility was dirty and the staff unfriendly. We agreed to keep Mom at home and things went okay for a couple of years.

As the disease progressed, Mom became incontinent and began to wander away from home. I knew then that we needed to take action. I called together the other family members, and we developed a plan. We divided up the tasks of researching all of the nursing homes that provide specialized care for persons with Alzheimer's disease, and we did a thorough search. We visited each one, and talked with the staff, and then we asked friends who had had experiences with these facilities what they thought. We decided on a facility that was bright and clean with staff that seemed caring and warm.

As a family we decided that we could no longer keep our promise to Mom because we could no longer provide the quality of care she required or keep her

safe. It was not an easy decision, but I know it was the
right one for Mom and for the entire family.

Betty, 54

Family Conflict during Caregiving

Caregivers who are only children think their jobs would be so much easier if they had siblings to help them. But caregivers who have brothers and sisters often claim siblings can be one of caregiving's greatest complications. The reason? While siblings can provide help, they may also provide very different opinions about how things should be handled.

Families tend to experience increased conflict when there is a caregiving crisis—a change in the loved one's physical or mental health, living situation, financial status. This may seem odd because we think that families pull together during crisis. Some families do pull together but some pull apart. Still others will pull together after an initial period of disharmony.

All change (good, bad, welcome, or unwelcome) creates stress, and when people feel stressed they need to release it. Some people recognize stress in themselves and handle it in ways that are not hurtful to themselves or others. Others, though, aren't even aware what they are feeling and end up dumping their emotions all over other family members. They may fly off the handle and become angry or say cruel things.

Understanding *why* conflict can occur is one thing, but doing something about it is something else. Here are some things to consider:

When you are tired or feeling fear, anger, grief, or sadness, you are more emotionally vulnerable and more likely to get hooked into a conflict. This is when you want to take steps to reestablish your emotional equilibrium. When you do this, you will be less sensitive to the criticism of your family members and less likely to lash out and say things you might regret later.

Think about things that help you reduce your stress level, then do them. Your list will be unique but could include going for a walk, listening to quiet music, talking to a friend, or watching a funny movie.

During caregiving crises, family members often spend more time together than they usually do. This can trigger old behavior patterns and lead to increased conflict. Simply getting away from each other for a little while can help.

Focus on only what absolutely must be taken care of at this time. Some things can probably be delayed until the situation calms and everyone is feeling less stressed. Before engaging in a potentially heated discussion, ask yourself if it must be done now or if it could wait.

No matter how stressful the caregiving situation, it does not excuse bad behavior toward each other. If your family member behaves in a hurtful way, you will probably be better served by telling her so rather than keeping it inside. You may, though, choose to postpone talking with her about it until you are both feeling less stressed. Timing is important, too.

Finally, remember that crises eventually end, and things will return to a more calm state, although sometimes not exactly as they were before. Caregiving may just have ushered you and your sibling to a *new* normal.

―⏤⟨⟨⟩⟩⏤―

My father's stroke left him disabled, and making caregiving decisions with my sister and brother was about as disabling for me. We seemed to disagree about every detail when we had to decide on the best place for Dad to live. My brother tried to pull rank most of the time, being the eldest and the only son. I found myself wanting to shout at him that we were not kids anymore, and he was not in charge.

My husband suggested I take some time away, so I spent a weekend with my daughter and her family. I could feel myself becoming calmer and more focused. When I returned I went to visit Dad at the assisted living facility we were finally able to agree on. I was pleased to see him doing so well.

I called my sister and brother to meet me for lunch. This time we all seemed to have profited from being apart for a while. We decided to take up Dad's financial situation with a professional and then we would move onto the other areas that needed attention. I think my father sensed the different feeling as we visited him.

Families can be like the children I teach, scared and out of control when something bad happens. Time out of a bad situation can work wonders.

Lorraine, 52

Balancing Time between Kids and Caregiving

Do you ever feel like a sandwich? Caring for an aging loved one on one side and raising children on the other. You're torn, wanting to spend time with your children and with your aging loved one but feeling like you aren't giving either enough time or attention. It can feel like you are squeezed in the middle of everyone else's needs.

A little self-examination may be in order. Could you be your own worst enemy? Are you adding to the chorus demanding that you do more and more? If so, your first job is to silence that demanding voice and replace it with a gentler voice, one that doesn't add to your stress.

Next, consider creating some realistic expectations for yourself. Are you being realistic about how much you can do? You may be able to readjust your expectations easily, or it may be difficult for you. If you find that you are always running from one caregiving task to another or from your child's soccer game to your parents' house, you may not yet have mastered the art of realistic expectations for yourself. Try this: make your daily to-do list, then cut it back by one-third. While this may cause you some anxiety, you may find that you still can't get through your to-do list even in its reduced form. If this is so, cut it back again.

If you continue to have difficulty getting your expectations in line with the time you have to meet them, you might want to consider talking with someone else—your spouse or partner, a friend, a coach, a therapist. Have someone else help you figure out if your expectations of yourself are unreasonable.

Have a talk with your children and your aging loved one, if age and health conditions allow. If your children are old enough, you can bring them into the discussion about ways you can spend time with them and also assist your loved one. Help them be part of the solution by talking with them, and, if possible, have the discussion with your children and your loved one at the same time. You may be surprised at the positive reaction you get. You may find that your loved one and your children make fewer demands once they understand how you are being squeezed.

Remember, you don't have to do this alone. There may be other family members, friends, agencies, and businesses who can reduce your workload so that the time you spend with your children and your loved one is less pressured and more enjoyable. If family members don't jump in to help you, then you might want to consider having a family meeting to discuss the situation and rebalance the workload.

Finally, children who are old enough to understand the situation don't need to be shielded from the challenges of caregiving. You will find they benefit in ways you may not even imagine by sharing in this experience with you. So, as much as possible, make it a family affair.

My parents had been living with us for the past three years because they were no longer able to take care of themselves. I am a stay-at-home mom with twin teenage daughters. After much discussion, I agreed to have Mom and Dad move in with us because I did not work outside the home. These last three years have been the most hectic time of my life, trying to balance the needs of my parents for medical care and attention with the usual needs of young teenagers. My husband took over with my parents and the kids when he got home from work, so we rarely had an evening to sit down and talk or watch TV together. The stress on me began to show; I had headaches all the time and felt guilty that I shortchanged either my parents or my girls and husband.

One day, I called everybody together and told them of my stressful and guilty feelings. My parents were very understanding and agreed to ask other family members to take them to doctor appointments and out to the senior center to play cards. My daughters had just gotten their driver's licenses, and they made a schedule for driving their grandparents to some of their activities. On those days, I got double relief and was able to do some things for myself. They even planned an early evening activity with their grandparents so my husband and I could go out for dinner together.

I am still the main organizer with both parents and the girls, but I now get a break from time to time, which gives me the energy to keep going. My headaches have disappeared.

Fran, 51

When Friends Disappear

One of the hardest parts about an aging loved one's illness or disability is that his or her long-time friends often disappear— sometimes slowly, sometimes quickly. This can magnify the caregiver's own feelings of loss and isolation.

Sloane's wife was a very social person with many friends. Yet when she had a serious stroke most of those friends eventually stopped visiting or calling. Always vivacious and social, his wife could only speak a few words after the stroke. Many of her friends didn't know how to behave around her; she had become a different person than the one they knew. Their contact was reduced to a Christmas card or a call once or twice a year. It was very difficult for Sloane, too, as the main caregiver. Her loss of friends became their loss of friends.

It's hard to understand why old, dear friends can simply disappear when a friend becomes ill or disabled. Some fear illness themselves and don't want to be reminded of the possibility, or they do not know what to say to a terminally ill friend. Others may have been caregivers at one time and/or fear having to be a caregiver for their own loved ones.

Whatever the reason, be open about how you feel. Let friends know that your aging loved one (and perhaps you) misses seeing them. "Mary and I really miss the time we used to spend with you and Joan."

Be empathic about how difficult this may be for them. "I know it is tough for you to see Mary like this. The changes can make it hard to have the same kind of friendship as before." Giving people the opportunity to talk about it will sometimes make it easier for them to feel comfortable around their longtime, but changed, friend.

Suggest specific things that your loved one can still do with friends, with or without you. Contact often breeds comfort with the physical and cognitive changes that accompany illness or disability, so create opportunities for your loved one's friends to have easy interactions—stopping by for a cup of coffee or lunch or sitting on the patio listening to the birds.

Teach friends how to behave around your loved one. "Mary isn't able to talk as well as she used to, but she still loves to be part of the conversation. She can still answer Yes or No." Model the behavior; show them how it's done. The more comfortable you are in the situation the more likely they are to be comfortable.

Be careful not to make friends feel guilty. Recognize that some people will never be able to adjust to the changes, but it does not mean they don't care about you and your loved one.

Even when friends disappear, you don't need to go it alone; support is available from people who understand what you and your loved one are facing. So go ahead and reach out for support and connection; you'll find that new friends await you.

Mom was 83 when her Parkinson's got so bad she could no longer leave the house. She had always been active—bridge, book groups, tennis—well into her seventies. Confinement has been very difficult for her. I called or visited her every day and soon realized I was her only visitor. I could see her becoming melancholy, but she did not complain.

I decided to make a few calls and see if I could encourage her friends to visit. It turned out that several of them had tried to come, but when Mom said no, they had not persisted. I arranged a meeting with three of her closest friends, and we talked about Mom's physical limitations and her embarrassment about her tremors. We also discussed the possible discomfort they might feel around her and how best to handle that.

*We planned activities in her home that she could
do with them—watching movies, reading books, reminiscing. The three friends arranged a schedule, and now
Mom sees somebody at least twice a week.
Friends stop visiting, I believe, because they don't
know how to respond to the changes. All they need is a
little help in finding new ways to relate to their dear
old friend.*

Marie, 60

My Family Doesn't Talk about That

There are *taboo* subjects in every family, things you know are
not open for discussion. As a caregiver, you may find this particularly tough because decisions or plans need to be made
that may involve one of your family's taboo topics.

You may find you need to talk with your aging loved one
about a sensitive subject—for example, his or her living will or
what type of funeral arrangements he or she wants. Or, you
may have to discuss a sensitive subject with another family
member, like future care plans, financial issues, or division of
caregiving responsibilities.

What are the best ways to approach talking about sensitive
subjects? Here are some tips.

▶ Talk about the issue in short conversations, one topic at
a time. This is one of the best ways to deal with subjects
that are hard to discuss. The temptation may be to discuss everything at once so you can get it over with.
However, you will find the quality of the discussion is
better if you break the issue down into several smaller
talks. One of the best ways to know when it is time to
stop talking about a subject is when the other person
disengages by fidgeting, looking away, or walking away.
It is then time to take a break.

► Acknowledge that the subject is difficult to talk about; that, alone, can make people feel more comfortable. Explain why you believe it is so important to discuss the topic, despite its sensitivity.

► Explain, up front, exactly what you think needs to be discussed, creating an informal agenda. People are generally more relaxed when they know the parameters of the discussion rather than wonder what is coming next.

► Some people do better if they are made aware when a difficult discussion is going to take place. For example, if your sibling avoids discussing care arrangements for your mother, you might say to him, "I think we need to talk with Mom about options for her care. If she is willing, would you be available Tuesday?" This usually works better than just launching into the topic with no warning, which can make some people feel as though they have been ambushed.

► If it's appropriate, remind family members this is a gift they are giving you. This is especially relevant in discussions with your aging loved one about future care or funeral and burial plans. You can explain to your loved one that you would have peace of mind when the time comes if you know you are fulfilling his or her wishes.

► If your family is still unable to talk about taboo topics, you might want to consider having a professional facilitator help your family through the discussions.

―――

Over the past few years, I've found the hardest part of taking care of Dad has been dealing with all the different family styles and personalities. Let me give you an example of what I mean. Dad had always kept his finances private, but when his mental functioning began to decline, I knew that we needed to take over that responsibility for him.

My two sisters said we would be intruding in Dad's business and we should just let things go until Dad died. Our discussions about this topic always ended up in an argument and no action. Finally, I asked our minister if she would sit with the family and help us to discuss the issue in a constructive way. I asked the other family members if they would go along with this plan, and they agreed. We set a date that was acceptable to all, and we all acknowledged that we wanted to do the best thing for Dad.

The meeting went very well. The minister, who had helped other families in this way, made sure that everyone was heard, and she did not express her own views until the end. Then, she said that it would be a mistake to let the finances languish. We owed it to Dad, who worked hard for that money, to be sure that it was invested correctly and that any outstanding transactions were completed. We moved forward as stewards of Dad's finances, all agreeing it was the right thing.

Lizanne, 34

What Should I Tell the Grandchildren?

Just how do you explain a complicated illness to a child? How do you help him or her understand that Grandpa has changed in ways he can't do anything about? How much do you say and what do you leave out?

The most important thing is to direct conversation to the age and maturity of the child. Young children who are not yet able to think abstractly need information that is presented in a concrete and concise manner. That does not mean they should be shielded from knowing about Grandpa's or Grandma's condition, it just means they should be told the information in simple language with short explanations. For example, when a grandparent has Alzheimer's disease and it has progressed to a point that memory loss is obvious even to a small child, you can say, "Grandpa sometimes has a hard time remembering things. But even when he can't remember things he still loves it when you visit and draw pictures for him." The child's reaction and questions will guide you as to whether or not you need to say anything more.

Learning a grandparent has a progressive and incurable disease can be difficult and painful. Yet we know that children develop coping skills to deal with life's difficult situations not by being shielded from learning them, but by exercising their coping muscles. Just as with physical muscles, emotional muscles only develop with use. Instead of trying to protect children from life's inevitable pain, we should teach them it's okay to feel sad and angry. By making it comfortable and safe for them to talk about how they feel, we can help them work through the painful feelings.

Older children are better able to process the information about what is happening to the grandparent. Talking with them allows you to open the conversation about how this news makes them feel. You can share your feelings about what is happening with your parent, as a way of giving your child permission to talk about his or her own feelings. Be cautious about not saying too much, but sharing that you, too, are sad and angry can validate their feelings. Your children will give you your cue about whether or not they want more information or want to talk more about their feelings.

The best strategy is to just let your children know you are open and available to talk if and when they want to. Remember, children are quick to sense an adult's discomfort about discussing difficult things. So make sure you mean it before you proclaim openness.

When my Dad was diagnosed with colon cancer, my son, Matt, was 13 years old. At first, I tried to hide everything about the illness from Matt. When I was growing up, kids were not told much about family matters like illness, and they were often excluded from participating in the funeral when a dear one died. Somehow, it just didn't feel right to me to try to exclude Matt. I also sensed that he knew something was wrong, but he was afraid to ask questions. I decided to do it differently from the way I was raised and to follow my instinct to share with Matt.

So we chose a good time to sit down, the three of us, and we told him the whole story about the cancer and the plans for treating it. We did not go into much detail, but we did give him the basic, straight story. Of course, we both were full of optimism about the outcome of the treatment and that Grampa would be fine.

Matt seemed clearly relieved to know the "secret." He had known that there was trouble, and he wondered what it was. Then, we gave him the chance to ask questions, which turned out to be about things important to him, like who was going to drive him to soccer practice and could he still go to camp this summer. We all agreed to have a weekly meeting when we would update him on what was happening and how we would handle tasks while Grampa was in treatment. Our session ended with a big group hug that made it all worthwhile.

Vera, 42

CHAPTER FIVE

Circle 4: **Relationships with the Greater Community**

ONE OF THE GREATEST CHALLENGES OF CAREGIVING is that it is added to an already busy life. Before becoming caregivers, people may be juggling the roles of spouse/partner, parent, employee or employer, or member of a faith community or other community groups. Then they become caregivers and have to figure out how to add this new role into the mix of all of the other roles in their lives. And in each of these roles there are relationships with people who impact and are impacted by the very consuming role of caregiving. Thus the challenge is not just about balancing roles; it is about managing relationships.

This chapter on the fourth circle out from the center is a good reminder of just how far into our lives the impact of caregiving reaches. In this chapter you will find tips for juggling the many roles you play and tips for better managing the relationships you have in each of these roles. Just remember as you read these tips that even professional jugglers drop a ball sometimes. And when they do, they know that all they have to do is reach down, pick it back up, and begin juggling again. And soon they will get their rhythm back.

How Can I Balance Working and Caregiving?

If you are one of the many caregivers who holds down a full- or part-time job, you already know that *balance* is the magic word. Balancing the demands of your job, your own family, and your caregiving responsibilities takes real skill. Then, we add in your need to take care of yourself, and you may say—impossible! Think of yourself as the bank account. You have to make deposits in order to have something to withdraw. So, self-care becomes critical if you want to effectively balance all the other aspects of your busy life. Maybe you are lucky enough to work for a company that provides some support for caregivers. These employers know they will benefit the bottom line if they can help workers find ways to get the job done while still caring for loved ones who are ill. Even if your company does not have formal programs to help you, here are some ideas that might help you balance work and caregiving.

► Consider talking to your supervisor about your caregiving situation. It is usually better that he or she understands if you need to come in late or take some time for medical appointments. This may be a difficult step to take. Perhaps you fear it will affect your job security or career prospects. If so, you might first consider checking your company's personnel manual or other human resources publications to learn and understand your company's policies. Having this information can boost your confidence when you talk with your supervisor. You may be surprised how supportive your supervisor and coworkers can be when they learn how you are supporting your loved one. Your company may also appreciate your honesty and your sense of responsibility toward your job and your loved one.

► Let your boss know that you are committed to getting your work done. Ask for some flexibility in your hours or offer to do the work outside of regular hours.

► Let your coworkers know that you appreciate the help they give you in balancing job and home. You could offer to take on an extra assignment for them when you do have the time.

► Make necessary calls for medical appointments or other caregiving business during your lunch or coffee break. Avoid interrupting your work.

► Find one activity every day that you do for yourself to relieve some of the stress. Take a short walk or a hot bath, call a friend and talk about other things besides caregiving.

► Remember to eat well, get enough sleep, and fit in some exercise. Keep that bank account full.

I felt so guilty about how my caregiving for my elderly mother had begun to interfere with my job. I had tried to hide my stress at work and act as if everything was normal. One day my boss called me in and said he knew what I was dealing with at home, and he wanted to try to make things easier for me. I was able to tell him about the pressure I was feeling.

We were able to figure out some flextime for my schedule and he suggested that I could do some work from home. I am so grateful for such a supportive boss.

Beatrice, 45

Reaching Beyond Your Network

What do you do when you've recruited family and friends but still need more help? There are still tasks to do and no time to do them. This is when you have to reach beyond your inner circle to a wider network of friends and acquaintances.

Melinda was stretched so thin that she knew she had to have new helpers to spend some time with her ailing father. She put a note on her church bulletin board asking for members to volunteer to spend one or two hours with her dad. She posted a calendar for volunteers to fill in. Melinda was delighted to find that many members had signed up, some offering to help one time and some taking a regular shift once or twice a week.

At first Melinda worried that her father would see this regular appearance of visitors as an intrusion into his privacy. In most cases, the opposite was true. He enjoyed having new people around to stimulate and fuss over him and listen to his stories.

Janelle had a different situation. She was concerned that her husband, who was quite weak, would resist having a health care aide come in at night. He was quite unsteady on his feet, particularly at night when he woke up to go to the bathroom. After just a few nights, Janelle's husband said he was actually relieved that someone was there to help him as he, himself, was afraid of falling down.

If you are part of a faith-based organization, you can, like Melinda, post a note requesting help. Your local senior center or community center may also have posting options. You may be surprised at how willing people are to lend a hand. There are many things beyond hands-on caregiving that could serve to lighten your load. Enlist help:

- ► Programming a new digital phone or setting up the television near your loved one's bed.

- ► Doing yard work—mowing the grass, weeding the garden, pruning the shrubs, fertilizing the lawn.

- ► Doing small home repair jobs. One neighbor cut down the legs on the chess table for his bedridden friend so they could resume their weekly games.

► Preparing food. When someone brings a dish that appeals to Melinda's father, whose appetite has been waning over the past few months, Melinda makes a fuss over the dish. She is so complimentary that the cook often offers to bring that dish again.

► Returning your books to the library or picking up a book for you, walking the dog, running an errand. Check the library to see if they have any special services for homebound patrons.

We often hesitate to ask for things from people we do not know well. But many are willing and are happy to know specific ways to help. Having additional help allows you to concentrate your energies on caregiving tasks. It also frees your time so you can be with your loved one and just enjoy him or her.

When my wife, Ethel, was crippled by rheumatoid arthritis last year, I had no problem asking our son and his family to pitch in and help us. My sister, Freida, lives nearby, so I recruited her to come each week and fix Ethel's hair and give her a manicure.

As Ethel's condition worsened, I found that I just did not have enough hands to do everything that needed to be done. My son and his wife were helpful, but they both have full-time jobs and their kids have a thousand activities besides school.

I knew I needed more help, so I contacted my Rotary chapter. I have been a member for many years, and they were very responsive to my need for help. One friend organized a schedule for fellow Rotarians to come almost every day of the week. They helped with yard work and handyman projects. The wives did a

*batch of cooking for us and took shifts with Ethel to
read to her or just keep her company.
It couldn't have been better; this was just the extra
help I really needed.*

Franklin, 78

How Much Do I Tell?

When people ask you about your loved one, do you make a
quick assessment about how much to tell them? It's a bit like
one of our most common greetings: "How are you?" It's a
question that really begs a very short response: "Fine, and how
are you doing?"

You may have already scripted different responses about
your loved one depending on how much you think the person
wants to know or how much you are willing to tell him or her.
Rose usually starts with the ten-second version about her
husband: "He's doing pretty well. The doctors say that he is
holding his own. And I'm trying to take good care of myself
as well." She's found that most people will then be ready to
move on to other topics. If the person asks for more detail,
she gives it willingly.

Rose recognized the wisdom of such an approach by
observing her husband, a financial expert, answer questions
about the stock market. When people asked him what he
though the stock market would do, he would often give a
lengthy explanation of the economic trends, bond prices, and
consumer confidence. Most people, she noticed, just wanted
to know if the market would go up or down.

You have friends, relatives, and social acquaintances who
do want to know developments in your loved one's illness. An
easy way to communicate is to create a list of these contacts on
your email so you can send periodic reports. This way, you can

save phone calls and visits for those close friends and family whom you want to contact personally. If the phone calls become too much for you, you can ask one person to let others in your group know. You want to keep people informed so they can support you and your loved one, but you also want to protect yourself from spending all your time and energy communicating to others.

As caregivers, you are grateful for all the people who care about and want to know what is happening during this time of illness. Remember, though, that your top priority is conserving your energy to help support your loved one. Your friends and family will understand.

━━━━━

I am the caregiver for Aunt Nancy, who has a degenerative neurological disorder. People are very kind and solicitous about my situation. Not only do my friends want information, but Nancy's friends also want contact with me. As the requests for information increased, I became overwhelmed. Nancy's best friend, Kara, asked if she might help by communicating with Nancy's friends for me.

This has helped so much, and whenever Kara sends out an update, Nancy receives emails from friends with their own news and words of encouragement. I maintain my own contact with family and some close friends. But what an energy-saving system this has been, and it lets us determine the amount of information we want to share.

When someone asks, "How's Nancy?" I can keep it simple and don't feel bad about it at all. Caregiving is a profession in itself, and I'm learning new things every day.

Joan, 56

Many Hands

Have you ever thought, "Wouldn't it be great if someone would offer me just a little help now and then?" For many of us, help may be just around the corner—literally.

Geri-Lynn and her husband, Paul, moved when Paul's employer offered him a generous early retirement package if he was willing to move and finish his management job across the country in a new office. He accepted, and within weeks, they were living in a newly built home in a neighborhood filled with young families. Some of the neighbors brought cookies and muffins to welcome the couple, and in no time, they were both enjoying retirement. Paul and Geri-Lynn were youthful in spirit and began hosting cookouts and serving in their homeowner's association—life was full and retirement was looking grand.

One day while packing for a picnic, Paul experienced a stroke. He spent four weeks between the hospital and a rehabilitation center where he learned to speak again. The couple was told that Paul would need help with some daily living activities for the rest of his life. This devastated the couple, and the first year of caregiving for her husband flew by for Geri-Lynn. She found herself consumed by Paul's care, turning down invitations to neighborhood functions until she only felt a part of her own housebound community of two.

One morning, Geri-Lynn went out for the newspaper and greeted her friend Molly, from six doors down. They caught up for a time and as she was departing, Molly said, "If there's anything you ever need, just let me know." Before Geri-Lynn knew it, she blurted out, "I'd love it if you or Tom could spend some time with Paul while I go out for a bit . . . sometime." They were both a bit surprised; after all, Geri-Lynn had turned down Molly's offers every time since Paul's stroke. In fact, she turned several people down, not knowing what they could or should do. Now she knew.

Molly said they'd be happy to come by in the evenings or on weekends, just give them a little notice. After realizing how refreshed she felt after one short shopping spree all to herself, Geri-Lynn developed a network of neighborhood helpers whom she scheduled regularly to assist her with everything from shopping to cooking together to just sitting with Paul for a bit.

Just as Geri-Lynn learned to accept the compassion and love of others, you may be able to ask a friend or neighbor to pitch in to give you the breaks you need. Remember that "Many hands make light work," and others can lighten your workload and your mood, if you just ask. At the same time, your loved one will benefit from either rekindling relationships lost over time or building new ones.

—⟐⟐⟐—

Since Mom came to live with us, my life has been pretty much out of control. She is a dear, but she is gradually losing mental capacity and can't be left alone anymore. I have switched to the night shift at the hospital so I can be around to care for her during the day, and my husband is on call for her at night.

The only problem is trying to figure out when I can sleep! One day, I ran into my neighbor, and she commented on how tired I looked. She suggested I have some of the neighbors over for coffee one evening to see who might be willing to pitch in and help me. We had a schedule sheet and I asked for volunteers to come over and sit with Mom for two or three hour shifts so I could get some sleep. Many of my dear neighbors signed up right then and there. It seems that they were aware of my situation but just didn't know how to help. They were happy to be asked.

*Thank heavens my neighbor convinced me to ask
for help. Being rested makes it easier to handle work
and caregiving.*

Mary, 36

No One Is an Island

Just when we're convinced that caregiving is a one-person job,
a solitary situation, we hear something that reminds us that,
in fact, others have a deep need to share in your caregiving
experience.

Arlene lost her husband to colon cancer after caring for
him for more than five years. After his death, she gathered
together a small group of men her husband knew from
Kiwanis to share memories and stories and to seek some closure after the long caregiving experience.

Arlene described her close, loving relationship with her
husband. She shared her sadness that her husband had not
been able to share his feelings about his approaching death.
She had tried many times to begin the dialogue, but she felt
that it was his choice to talk about it or not. Fortunately,
Arlene had a wonderful network of friends, so she was able to
share her feelings and sense of uncertainty about how his disease would progress and what the future might bring.

At the gathering of her husband's friends from Kiwanis,
one of them told her that his relationship with her husband
went well beyond just the usual friendly banter at the meetings.
He said that they had had many deep conversations, which
included a sharing of their current problems and lots of support and caring for each other. Arlene learned that her husband
had, in fact, shared feelings about the disease and the pain with
his Kiwanis friend. He was able to reassure her husband that
today's medications would be able to manage the pain. Further,
her husband told his friend about his concerns for Arlene, how

she'd survive his death and manage without him. He also spoke of his gratitude for the life that he had lived for 75 years and his powerful love for Arlene and their son.

Arlene realized at the gathering that her husband showed his love for her by revealing his fears and concerns to his friend from Kiwanis. He wanted to protect her. She was relieved to know that he had been able to let out his feelings to someone. She was grateful that there had been another person to share the emotional difficulties of her husband's illness and death.

So, you may not be the only caregiver your loved one needs. He or she needs to have other people with whom they can talk about concerns they don't mention to you. You can make sure that your loved one has the opportunity to reach out to others—a close friend, family member, counselor, or spiritual leader.

I have been a constant companion for my wife, Anne, for the past two years since her heart condition got worse, leaving her homebound. I love her dearly, and I don't mind staying home most of the time, although I did miss playing poker with my buddies at the senior center on Tuesday evenings. When Anne and I talk about her illness she always says she is getting better, and she will soon be able to get back to her regular activities. I know that is not really likely, but I don't want to burst her bubble of optimism. Lately, she has insisted that I go out with my poker buddies. Our grandson Todd now comes to be with her on Tuesday evenings.

I had a chance to talk with Todd one day, and he told me that when he visited, his grandmother told him how worried she was about me and how I would cope when she died. It seems that she was willing to tell him that she knew her health was deteriorating, but she didn't want to talk to me about that. She told Todd that she wanted me to stay involved in outside activities so I would have a life when she passed.

Now, when I talk to Anne, I tell her about my activities at the senior center and I make sure that she knows I am keeping in touch with folks. It makes her feel better to know that I am and will be okay.

Terence, 82

Get a Life

It often happens that chronically ill people become less and less able to participate fully in life's activities. They gradually give up much of their connection with the world as they knew it. It may be the physical stamina is gone or it may be a psychological withdrawal from social interaction.

One loving husband described how his wife became nearly a shut-in as her emphysema forced her to give up most physical activity. She had attended a regular pulmonary exercise class at the local wellness center for five years, until her doctor recommended that she stop because it was too hard on her system. The wellness center staff held a graduation ceremony for her with a certificate and cards full of well wishes.

We can imagine how easily depression can set in when one is chronically ill, how the person could choose to withdraw from all social contacts. William was sad himself seeing his aging father sitting home all day watching television. He resisted the tendency, though, to nag his father, even when the constant noise from the television got on his nerves. William got creative. He bought comfortable earphones for his father to wear so the noise in the room was minimized. Then, William brought movies to watch with his father, ones they both could enjoy. As the caregiver, it's important to keep your perspective and not lose yourself as you care for your loved one. It is critical for you to set limits and do only as much as you can reasonably do. When you feel that you are no longer addressing your own needs, it's time to step back and identify those people, groups, and activities in your life that can form your network of support. Make a list of people and activities beyond your family and close friends who can help you. You might want to consider neighbors, counselors, community groups, clergy or members from a faith-based group, and service organizations as a starting point.

When my husband's disability severely limited his mobility, I left my job and found contract work that I could do at home. I also gave up my volunteer work and dropped out of my bridge group, which had played together for many years. I didn't really know what a caregiver was supposed to do, but I assumed that I was meant to be there for my husband all day every day. It worked for a while and then I began to feel like an invalid myself.

One day, a bridge buddy stopped by because I had stopped returning her phone calls. She convinced me that I needed to stay involved in some activities outside the home, or I might grow to resent the situation and not be as effective in caring for my husband. Her words did make sense to me.

We then figured out together how I could rejoin the bridge group, even meeting at my house sometimes. She offered to rally my friends to come and visit my husband so I could get out a couple times a week. I didn't

go back to my volunteer work because I felt like I was
doing a different kind of volunteering at home now.
The funny thing about the change was that my
husband felt better about my going out. He had felt
secretly guilty that I thought I had to be around all the
time. It was a relief to him as well.

June, 61

Making Decisions about Work

If you are balancing work and caregiving, you already realize how important it is to make decisions that will facilitate your life. Sandra Day O'Connor made such a decision when she stepped down from her position as United States Supreme Court Justice to spend time with her husband, who suffers from Alzheimer's disease.

It is safe to say that all who hold outside jobs experience difficulty trying to figure out how to keep their jobs moving forward with the constant interruptions from their loved ones at home. There is clear consensus around one point: it is best to share your situation with your employer and figure out together how to manage your work and home responsibilities.

If you try to keep your caregiving a secret, your employer and fellow staff members may think that you don't care enough about the job on the days when you must be late or you are distracted from your work by the problems at home. If you do explain the situation, you may be surprised by their supportive attitude and willingness to help.

Julia's company wanted her to take her allowed three-month medical leave when she told them about her husband's cancer diagnosis. She thought it through and realized that she would rather continue working while her husband was still functioning pretty well. Julia wanted to save that leave time until later, when her husband was closer to the end and would need her full time.

Elizabeth's situation was different. She had a high-powered job that involved overtime and travel. When her mother was diagnosed with Alzheimer's disease, Elizabeth realized that her priorities would need to shift. She needed the flexibility to deal with her mother's issues as they came up. Her job would not allow her to drop everything and to run home and deal with crisis. Elizabeth began interviewing for a new job, telling prospective employers up front that her primary concern at this point in time was her mother. She found a less-pressured job that allowed her to work from home and required less travel.

Nobody said that caregiving is easy. To do it well means looking at your own lifestyle and work to determine what is right for you and your loved one. Sandra Day O'Connor made a decision that surprised the nation but was right for her and her husband. And the same is true for you. Take the time for those decisions that will make your and your loved one's lives work as well as possible.

My husband, Ron, and I were on our way up in our careers. Then, my father had a massive heart attack and needed help from me. During that time, I tried so hard to keep it all going, with my job and our young children's school and activities. I felt I had to handle everything and only I could do it. Not wanting anyone to see my vulnerability, I would go out on the porch and cry.

When I came down with a serious throat infection, my doctor asked about my situation at home. I told him about my work and family demands and my father's condition and limitations. He referred me to a heart attack support group for family members. If I had to name just one thing I learned in the group, I would have to say balance. *I realized that I had not taken care of myself. I had put my job, Ron, the kids, and my dad on one side of the seesaw and me on the other. Looking at it that way, I could see that balance would have been impossible.*

I've since made changes all around me. I talked things over with my supervisor, and we worked out a schedule with fewer hours and working at home more. I asked the children to take on more responsibility around the house. Ron has been very supportive of my daily personal *time. My life is now manageable, my health is good, and my dad is recovering nicely. I'd say we are finally in balance.*

Dee, 42

Need Help? Try Going Back to School

You may have recognized that you and your loved one need some help managing the time it takes to do all that caregiving requires. But where do you find someone who is willing to come by, even for a couple of hours, so you can shop, get your hair cut, or just go out for a walk?

Besides your family, friends, and neighbors, there are trusting people all around you to help. Go to the local high school, community college, or university. They all provide opportunities for teens and young adults to do community volunteer work. If you have a child between the ages of 16 and 21, then you have ready access to a dozen or more compassionate young adults who are eager to serve you.

Gretchen saw how tired her mother became while caring for her grandfather, who had had a stroke the year before. That's in addition to the usual care Mom took of her teenage daughter and son. Gretchen belonged to her high school's Key Club. Their mission is to serve, to build character and leadership. When Gretchen asked if there was any way for the Key Club to help her family, the teacher answered with a resounding Yes! Soon, a meeting was held between the teacher and Gretchen's mother, and they determined the times that a student would come once per week to provide a break for Mom. There was a regular routine with kids coming in and talking, playing games, or watching a movie with Gretchen's grandfather. Her mother listed important notes and numbers in the kitchen in case there was a need for them to contact her during the short time she would be away. They arranged for the students to come after lunch on a weekend when the primary caregiving duties had already been completed.

This success story is just one of many that show how to make some simple caregiver dreams come true. You can contact other student organizations, such as Volunteer Services (located on most college campuses), to get the names of responsible young adults to be companions to your loved one for the short time you need away from your caregiving duties.

———

I have been caring for my mother, who has chronic obstructive pulmonary disease, for the past four years. With my background in social work, I know how important it is to ask for help. There are times, however, when I feel like I have already asked everyone I know, and they have given me lots of help and are feeling kind of burned out themselves. At that point, I know I need to find some new sources. I gave myself an A+ for creativity when I thought of contacting some former classmates of mine. We had met after the class ended as a support group for several years, but stopped meeting just a few years ago. Well, I contacted all those women and told them about my difficulties with caregiving for my mom.

It was like a miracle. They sprang into action and talked to each other about how they could support me. The ones who still lived in town stopped by and offered to visit with Mom, take her shopping, and even to her rehab appointment. Others who had moved away sent funny DVDs and videos for us to watch. One woman even sent me a gift certificate for a massage.

The lesson I learned from this wonderful experience is that there are many more resources than we think are available to us.

Mary, 45

CHAPTER SIX

Circle 5: **Working with Professionals**

S OME CAREGIVERS BELIEVE THEY, and perhaps other family members, should be able to provide all the care their loved one needs. And furthermore, they believe that if they aren't able to do this without professional assistance, they have somehow failed as a caregiver.

I think these beliefs place unnecessary stress on the caregiver. Trying to provide all of the care alone, or as a family, may not be the best strategy if the goal truly is taking excellent care of someone else as well as excellent care of ourselves.

Instead, I think we as caregivers need to think of professionals as our partners in providing excellent care for our loved ones and in reducing our burden. These professionals might be doctors and other health care providers, hospice workers, staff at an assisted living facility, or home care workers. They are our team members in keeping our aging loved one as healthy and as independent as possible.

How can we best approach and work with this team? In this chapter you will find ideas for doing just that: ideas for working more effectively with professionals to benefit your loved one ... and you!

Much More Than Another Set of Ears

One of your important caregiving roles is helping your loved one deal with doctors and the medical community. In this situation, you provide more than just another pair of ears as the doctor explains the condition and suggests actions to take. Your loved one may not be able to listen with objectivity to the diagnosis and treatment plans. When the illness is life threatening, your loved one may be fearful and may misinterpret what is said. If your loved one has dementia or is too sick to take part in the discussion, you must take the lead in dealing with the doctor.

In these situations, we hope the doctor responds in a tactful and effective way. A sensitive doctor might speak directly to the patient, knowing that he or she is really talking to the caregiver. If you feel that the doctor is not responding with appropriate respect for your loved one, you have the right to ask privately that your loved one be included in the discussion, to the extent possible.

Doctors are naturally caring, but time constraints sometimes prevent them from being sensitive enough or taking the time to be sure that the patient understands the information and has the opportunity to ask questions. Making sure that you and your loved one leave the appointment with all the information you need may take some thought and organization beforehand.

Prepare a set of questions. You might do some research about the illness and list symptoms that concern you or reactions to medications. You could ask the nurse to show your questions to the doctor before he or she sees you and your loved one.

In general, nurses and other health care professionals can be great allies. They are often able to explain things in a way that you and your loved one can understand and will repeat things you may have missed that the doctor said.

While the doctor usually knows what is best for the patient, sometimes your loved one and you know better how he feels or what his needs are. If something does not make sense, ask about it. Do not hesitate to let the doctor know any personal information that may affect the treatment plan. Of course, with a sense of trust and comfort, you and your loved one must agree on what you plan to share.

Doctors can be most effective when patients are well informed, and you and your loved one deserve to have all your questions answered and your fears addressed. Your concerns need to be the doctor's concerns, no matter how busy he or she may be. You can be polite but firm. If you have been reluctant to be direct with doctors, you may be surprised how your courage builds as you practice advocating for your loved one.

In dealing with the medical community, you can be much more than just another pair of ears. Taking an active role in forming a partnership with the doctors can help you make the very best of the situation.

—⏤⏥⏤—

My wife Betsy's particular type of cancer made it difficult for us to get the answers we wanted to get from our doctor. I had worked in the field of information technology, so I used the Internet to search out all that I could about the types of treatment that were being done throughout the country. At first, Betsy was uncomfortable presenting our questions based on my research to her doctor, and sometimes, I think she was somewhat distracted in our meetings with him.

It turned out he was very receptive to our presenting this information, and his openness helped tremendously in our communication. He seemed very pleased that we came into the appointment with questions

*written down. We felt as though we were working
as a team.*

*When we are in his office, I make sure that Betsy
always feels she is the decision maker. We're fortunate
that we don't feel rushed and that we have the doctor's
full attention. When I sense that Betsy is distracted, I
ask the doctor to repeat what I think she might not
have understood. I know we are the consumers and
have the right to expect good care. I am so glad I can
be there for Betsy as her advocate.*

Tim, 65

Three Things to Know about Assisted Living

Caregivers faced with finding an assisted living option for a
loved one may feel as though they've stepped into a foreign
land, one with a new language and new rules, assumptions,
and unknowns. The challenge can be amplified if you are providing care from a distance.

There are three questions to ask as you explore the assisted
living options for your loved one: is there a sense of partnership between the staff and patients, do they practice collaborative problem solving, and who is the head of the care team?

In a partnership, participants are committed to the success
of the project. As you evaluate different facilities, be alert to
each staff's attitude about forming a partnership with you and
your loved one. In a sense, your loved one will be living in
someone else's house, so building alliances is important to his
or her quality of life. Trust your instincts if you feel adversity
rather than alliance on your visit.

Collaborative problem solving progresses naturally in a
partnership. During your selection process, ask the staff about
problems they've seen and how they solved them. Listen care-

fully for beliefs, assumptions, and processes that suggest collaborative problem solving is practiced or is at least a possibility. It is critical that all members of the partnership communicate. Problems can arise when that doesn't happen, and often the first impulse is to find fault. If a problem that concerns your loved one's care develops, you will become the coach on behalf of him or her. It may become your responsibility to sort out and correct the issue. This may involve asking for a meeting with everyone involved, to understand and work together to come to a solution. It may help to write down the agreed-upon solution so it is available to care providers on other shifts.

The leader of the care team is the person who will have the overall responsibility for your loved one's care. It is important to meet him or her on your visit. The care team leader will ensure that your loved one has a good care plan and that the staff who deliver it are managed well. Ask if the care team leader is a full-time position. Things can slip through the cracks without a leader.

Forming a solid partnership, ensuring collaborative problem solving, and meeting the care team leader should be high on your checklist as you consider assisted living options for your loved one.

My family and I knew it was time to consider an assisted living facility for our mother. Dad died many years ago, and Mother's done very well. Now, though, her condition has deteriorated, and she requires more help than could be given at home.

My sister and I work in the health field and selected two well-known facilities in our area to consider. What we didn't know were their inner workings.

*We interviewed the director at each place and then
asked to talk to some staff.*

*We quickly saw a dysfunctional system in one. The
staff didn't seem to be very clear about how to handle
certain problems when we posed questions about some
of our mother's needs. The reason for the concern
became obvious when we talked to the head nurse,
who oversaw the care team. She did not have the kind
of experience that was necessary to manage the staff.*

*Our decision was made easier when we visited the
second facility. From the director on down, things
seemed to have a flow and focus in a way that was
very clear. Still, my sister and I knew that we would be
a regular part of Mother's care.*

*It's not an easy move, placing a family member in
this kind of facility, but it can be so much better if you
do your homework. Don't just trust the brochures; find
out for yourself what makes each facility tick.*

Annette, 62

Ready, Set, Hesitate

One of the most agonizing issues that caregivers deal with is
having to seek outside help for their loved ones. *Outside help*
doesn't mean scheduling neighbors, friends, or other family
members to spend time with your loved one, it means finding
professional, paid help. This may be arranging for assistance in
the home, or it may mean moving your loved one to a care
facility. Situations vary, and only you will know when, or if, it
is time to call for professional assistance.

Abby is entering her eighth year of caring for her husband,
who has Alzheimer's disease. He is relatively healthy, sits all day
without communicating, and is not incontinent or aggressive
in his behavior. Every one of Abby's friends as well as her adult

children, who live in other states, believe that she should place her husband in a care facility for Alzheimer's patients. She is just not ready. Abby wants to keep her husband at home until his symptoms worsen to the extent she can no longer manage. She does not expect her children to disrupt their lives to care for their father. They, in turn, respect her decision and give her as much support as they can.

Brad's partner is dying from cancer, but the doctors say it could be as many as six months. There is adequate long-term care insurance to allow him to hire full-time help to stay with his partner. But Brad has chosen to provide the care by himself. Why? He has trouble articulating his reasons to friends and family, who all advise him to get the help. Like Abby, Brad is just not ready. He feels that bringing in outside help would be uncomfortable for his partner, and he feels they would lose their privacy and sense of intimacy during these last, precious months together.

Another family is struggling to care for their aging father, who had once exacted the promise they would never put him in an institution. His daughter Lenore left a good job with benefits to care for her father. This family is not ready to abandon their promise, although it was made at a time when neither they nor their father could have foreseen how difficult care would become or what sacrifices would be required. In hindsight, Lenore and her sister and brothers wished they had instead promised their father they would *always* make sure he had the best possible care for whatever situation he was in.

If Abby, Brad, and Lenore tell us anything, it is that every situation is different and each family must decide for themselves what is best for them and their loved one. Friends and neighbors may offer their perspectives, but when it comes down to it, the family caregivers must decide when they are ready.

I thought I had made my decision about what was the right kind of care for my husband. His stroke had made him almost completely dependent on help from me and my son. Everyone had convinced me it would take too much to care for him at home. My son and my friends said I needed to have him admitted to a nursing facility. I reluctantly agreed that it was the best for all. When I tried to explain to Tom the need for this move, he became very agitated. I knew he understood what this change would mean.

I love Tom, and it broke my heart to think this was the only way. So I started to look into other options, such as home health services, companions, and visiting professionals. I realized we could afford to combine some of these services and work out a schedule that would allow me to relieve myself of the full pressure of Tom's care. I consulted my financial advisor, and he agreed that we could do this for a reasonable period of time. My heart and body told me this was the right decision for now.

I told Tom and was sure I had chosen the right road when he struggled to reach out his hand to hold mine. I'm aware that this plan may need to change in the future, but for now, I'm glad we chose this route.

Peggy, 82

What Can You Expect from the Facility's Staff?

Do you ever wonder just what you should expect from the staff caring for your loved one who is in a nursing home or other care facility? Can you ask a staff member to do or not do something? Is the way they are treating your loved one acceptable?

It's always best to ask specific questions and make specific observations before your loved one moves into a facility or becomes a participant in a specific program. To gain some insight, you can just watch staff interactions with the residents. Spend some time observing in a public area, like a lounge or dining room. Here are some things to watch for.

► Do the staff treat residents with dignity and respect? Notice how they talk to residents. Do they speak to them as adults or children? Do they listen to them and try to answer their questions or are they hurried and dismissive?

► Do the staff seem friendly to the residents? Are they kind? This will become evident as you observe the interactions.

► Are staff frantically running about, looking stressed? This can be normal sometimes, but shouldn't be all of the time. Do staff members have little or no time to interact properly with the residents? If so, the facility may be short staffed.

► Do the residents seem happy, and do they seem comfortable interacting with the staff?

Prior to your loved one moving into a residence or participating in a program, you should have an open and frank discussion with the appropriate staff person about what the staff does and doesn't do for and with the residents. You should also ask about how frequently they typically communicate with family members and how they keep family informed about significant issues or concerns. The more detailed information you get ahead of time, the less likely you are to be surprised once your loved one moves in. Finally, you should ask whom you should speak with if you ever have a concern about a staff member. It is helpful to explain that you are asking these questions because you want to work cooperatively with the staff to provide the best care possible for your relative.

If you didn't ask these questions before your relative moved into the facility, it isn't too late! You can have the discussion now. If you are unhappy with what you observe, you can schedule an appointment with the appropriate staff member. You may explain that you want to be clear on everyone's role, including your own, in the care of your loved one. Doing this as a family member who wants to be a cooperative member of the care team can help staff feel comfortable talking with you about other issues or concerns that might arise.

—◦◦◦—

Our family was dealt a very difficult blow when my sister Carol was diagnosed with Alzheimer's eight years ago and recently had to be placed in a special unit for advanced cases.

As the only family member who lived near enough, I visited her at least once a week. One day I heard a staff member speak to Carol as though she were a misbehaving child. I was angry but managed to keep my cool long enough to determine if this behavior was limited to my sister; it wasn't. Our family had researched this facility before Carol was admitted, and we felt we had made a good decision. I wasted no time going straight to the facility's director. She seemed solicitous but less than interested in what I had to say. She gave me a vague idea she would look into the situation.

Over the next months I saw no change or improvement. I talked to my brother and sisters and we agreed we needed to look elsewhere. This time we were much wiser. Not only did we speak with administrative staff but we watched staff and residents going about their daily activities. We spent time in the two best facilities, and last month, with much relief, we moved Carol.

*I am so glad we could improve Carol's quality
of life by providing her an environment where she is
treated with kindness and respect. The disease itself is
hard enough on us all; we did not need the added
stress of an unhappy living situation for our sister.*

Sarah, 63

What Is Hospice All About?

Perhaps the most difficult stage in caregiving is helping your
loved one prepare to die. But there are resources available to you.
Ralph's mother had stopped eating, just refused to do so.
She seemed to be preparing to die, yet she showed some alertness and even humor. After much discussion, Ralph and his
siblings decided to contact her doctor who made the necessary
referral and put them in touch with the local hospice office.
From that moment on, Ralph knew that they had done the
right thing.

Ralph and his family saw a team effort, including medical
assistance (home health aides and nurses), counseling for his
family and his mother (they were all encouraged to call and
talk at any time), and spiritual guidance from a chaplain. They
saw how the chaplain honored their mother's beliefs and provided appropriate support.

Hospice provided twice-weekly visits plus phone calls in
between. When Ralph's mother was close to death, hospice
staff stayed to make sure that she was as comfortable and pain
free as possible. When Ralph's mother passed away, the staff
even helped make the funeral arrangements.

Hospice provides literature and information to help families prepare for their loved one's death and to know what to
expect. They can help you know how to talk to your loved one,
how to let her go, and how to begin to handle all your feelings
about her passing.

People who have used the service usually speak highly of

hospice and their *live until you die* philosophy. Because there is often fear and discomfort around the issue of dying, it can be reassuring to have professional help to make your loved one's final days as peaceful as possible.

As my wife, Anne, was getting sicker, I began to realize that she would not be with me much longer. I was so confused about what to do. I spoke to the social worker who meets with patients and their families at the hospital. She explained what hospice care was, that there are some hospice facilities and hospice beds in hospitals but that most people receive their services at home. She also told me that hospice was not just for cancer patients but really for anyone who doctors said would probably die within about six months.

The social worker had the hospice representative contact me and he came to visit us within a few days. He did not rush us and answered all our questions and concerns. I was probably more resistant than Anne because I think she understood that I was going to need some extra help getting through these final months. So she was admitted to hospice care and it was the best thing we ever did. They were a very caring group of people who came to visit us regularly. In fact, they were as helpful to me as to Anne because they helped me prepare for her passing.

The team was right there with me through Anne's final days, and they supported me without being intrusive. I am so grateful for hospice and so glad I got the straight story about what their services were and were not.

George, 69

Hospice Help

It's not always easy to know when to call hospice, and it is not a one-sided decision. Your loved one's physician, other family members, and you, as the primary caregiver, all must reach consensus that it is time to begin hospice care.

The philosophy behind hospice is to improve the overall quality of life during the patient's remaining days and to support the family and caregiver. The hospice team seeks to calm fears of death for both the patient and the caregiver.

Reaching consensus about when to call hospice may not be easy; sometimes it is the patient who is less willing and sometimes it is another family member. While many connect hospice with impending death, some patients go in and out of hospice care as their conditions change and others outlive the six-month guideline.

Because hospice is a philosophy of care as well as a way of delivering care, it can be provided in different settings. It may be provided in a hospice facility, especially if the person is unable to be cared for at home or if he or she lives alone. However, this special care can also be provided in the patient's home or in a nursing home or a hospital. Nursing homes and hospitals often have designated areas for hospice patients.

Arlene shared with friends the comfort she received from hospice during the last months of her husband's life. She encouraged anyone in the same situation not to be afraid to consider this wonderful option. The hospice care team who came to her home included a social worker, nurse, nurse assistant to help with personal hygiene, dietician, and spiritual advisor. A physician served as an advisor to the care team, but he did not provide direct care. Medications related to the illness were also supplied.

For Arlene, the most difficult part of the initial meeting with the hospice team was having to sign a *Do Not Resuscitate* order. She had to face the reality of eliminating any emergency means to resuscitate her husband. Signing this document was an admission to herself that her husband was dying.

Arlene's husband never acknowledged that he knew what hospice meant, and he spoke throughout his final days of getting better and getting back out on the tennis court. Arlene had been able to convince him to begin hospice because she said that it was something *she* needed. The only downside to hospice, for Arlene, was the constant coming and going of team members. She realized she had to assert her and her husband's need for privacy and to limit the visits to what felt comfortable for them.

The goal of hospice is to facilitate a comfortable, meaningful life. The hospice team focuses on providing comfort care, which includes controlling pain, rather than curative treatment. Team members continue to help the family after the patient dies, including assistance in arranging a funeral or memorial service and bereavement counseling.

———

For more than a year, I had struggled with the idea of hospice for my mother, who had cancer. I felt as if I would be a traitor to her recovery if I even discussed hospice care with her. The fear of death was strong for both of us.

As Mother's condition deteriorated, I summoned the strength to bring up the idea of hospice with her. We talked about it for a few days, and we agreed how much we could gain by having hospice in our lives at such a difficult time.

After Mother died and all the activity ended, hospice was there to help me deal with her loss. Hospice enhanced the quality of her final days; the team's presence made all the difference for her and for me.

Mimi, 58

Communicating with the Doctor

An important aspect of caregiving is your support role when your loved one meets with his or her medical team of doctors, nurse practitioners, physician assistants, and nurses. Being able to communicate effectively with medical professionals can make a big difference in how your loved one handles the physical and the emotional aspects of these meetings.

In the beginning, it may be overwhelming to try to understand and remember all the details about the illness and the medicines, treatments, and potential side effects that are presented. In addition, you may not know the procedures in the health care center—who is responsible for which aspects, how to get your questions answered, or where to go to find things you need. It's a little like being a foreigner, trying to learn the language at a time when your loved one is not feeling very emotionally stable.

The reality of the health care system is that doctors see more patients than ever, and therefore the time they spend with a single patient has shortened. However, you have the right to as much information as you and your loved one need in order to make informed decisions. What is important to you must, in turn, be important to the doctor.

Knowing she would have to make the most of her father's appointment with the doctor, Lilly got herself organized. She didn't want to trust her memory, so she bought a small notebook that would fit into her purse and recorded questions she and her father had as they came up. Lilly also made notes to herself about how her father was feeling and acting and any medication-related issues. Because the illness caused her dad considerable pain, she made a one-to-ten scale to track the discomfort.

If dementia is a component of your loved one's condition, you would want to contact the doctor separately to discuss what to address, and not address, with him or her. Tell the doctor to what extent you are involved in making care decisions. Do you, for example, want to discuss possible approaches and decide with the team on the plan, or would you rather wait for the team to decide on the care path to take?

It is important to keep the medical team informed about your loved one's activities or over-the-counter medications or supplements, as they may affect the care plan.

My husband Lou's Parkinson's disease seemed to come on so rapidly that, at first, I felt confused about what was happening. I wanted to deny all the signs I saw in his everyday life. But, when I began to keep a daily journal, I finally saw what we were facing.

I scheduled an appointment with our long-time family physician. Before we went in, I spoke with the doctor and reviewed what I had been noticing about Lou's behavior. He suspected a probable diagnosis of Parkinson's disease and honored my wish to approach it slowly with Lou. I simply didn't want the doctor to talk about a diagnosis in our early appointments, until he was absolutely sure. I suppose I wanted to protect Lou as long as I could.

Now we are speaking openly during our doctor appointments and Lou seems to understand a good deal of what is said at the time. This worked well for us, and I am glad I decided to take it slowly with hearing the doctor's information.

Madeleine, 70

Respite Care

"Everybody needs a little time away..." So says the musical group Chicago, and while they aren't directing their words to caregivers, the sentiment applies. Time away—respite—may be a truer need for caregivers than for most other groups. Yet caregivers often hesitate to take a break from their duties, despite the fact they often provide care for a very long time— sometimes for many, many years.

Imagine working at a job for years without taking a vacation. Eventually your productivity would diminish and you would lose interest and simply burn out. The same thing happens to caregivers who never take a break; they become less effective in their caregiving roles and get less and less enjoyment from caregiving or from anything else in their lives.

Why, then, don't more caregivers take time off from their responsibilities? Here are some reasons that come up over and over. Perhaps you've had some of these same concerns.

► *There is no one available to take over my caregiving responsibilities.* Creativity is a necessity in this situation. There are formal respite programs at nursing homes and through home care companies, and, informally, respite care may be provided by friends. There may not be one person who can do all that you do, but you may be able to find several people to do different parts of what you do.

► *Even if there were someone to take care of my parent or spouse, no one can do it as well as I can.* This very well may be true. However, it is likely that there is a formal program or a friend who can keep your loved one safe and well cared for while you take a temporary break.

► *I could never afford to hire someone to take care of my loved one so that I could get away.* Again, this may be true, but explore the options before making a decision. Sometimes respite care is paid for by a government organization or insurance. And again, remember to be creative. You might find there are many people who would be willing to do part of the caregiving and wouldn't expect any payment for their contribution.

► *I'd spend the whole time away worrying about my loved one.* This is less likely if you feel comfortable with the person or people who are providing the care and if you establish some agreed-upon times to check in with your loved one and with the respite caregivers.

► *If my loved one died while I was gone, I'd never forgive myself.* If you need respite care for your relative, it is likely he or she is old and frail or sick. Therefore it is possible your loved one may die while you are gone, but it wouldn't be because you weren't there. It will be difficult whenever your loved one dies, and it is unlikely you will be able to prevent his or her death by never taking a break. However, it is best to prepare yourself for the possibility he or she might die when you are away. And you can add to your sense of comfort by having important closure conversations with your loved one before you go away.

I just assumed that I would be the sole caregiver for my 83-year-old mother, who has severe cardiac problems. The fact that I was exhausted most of the time, caring for her and my own family, didn't seem to register with anyone until I got sick myself.

My husband called a few of my mother's friends, and even a few of my own, and explained the situation. Well, the response was remarkable. One of my friends, a great organizer, offered to set up a visit, errand, and doctor appointment schedule, and she contacted the various people to fill in each slot for the next month. This dear friend also gave me a gentle but good talking-to about the need for me to get some respite from the total care of my mother. So I also called a home care company to arrange for respite care for a week in a few months when I'm going to take a vacation.

Now I am back to good health, and I am open to asking for some time for myself. Mother's friends are glad to continue helping, and they have also gotten others of her church friends involved. At first I was leery that they would forget to visit her or wouldn't know how to handle her, but actually, I think Mother is enjoying the many people who now come into her life.

So a word to the wise, you don't have to do it all. Take a break from caregiving and don't feel guilty about it. Then, when you return to your responsibilities, you will be refreshed and revived—better for you and your loved one.

Sally, 53

Adult Day Care Programs

Day-away or adult day care programs are a wonderful way to help your cognitively impaired loved one remain active while ensuring he or she is supervised and safe. These programs are in most communities and are something the busy caregiver might consider as both a means of activity for the loved one and a brief respite for him- or herself.

Jan's mother attended an adult day care program five days a week for several years and loved the activities. Prior to her stroke, Jan's mother was a very social and active person. Although her stroke caused her to lose much of her ability to speak and significantly limited her cognitive functioning, Jan's mother never lost her love of being with other people. The day care program provided Jan's mother wonderful socialization along with a full day of supervised activities that helped her maintain the physical and mental functioning she had left.

The program also gave Jan's father, the primary caregiver, a much-needed break and time to himself. Jan knew they would never have been able to keep her mother living at home if she did not attend the day care program.

As wonderful as adult day care programs can be, caregivers sometimes are troubled when the loved one becomes upset about the prospect of going to one, or just refuses to attend. This is a common reaction and does not mean he or she won't go, and maybe even enjoy, the program. As caregiver, you don't want to force your loved one to go, and you may be tempted to back away from the idea, even though the program is likely to benefit all family members.

Here are two ideas to make this situation easier for you and your loved one.

► Sometimes people are more willing to attend if they feel as though they are needed at the day care program. Many seniors who are attending adult day care programs believe they are volunteers in the program.

► If your loved one refuses to go—either before ever attending or after attending for a period of time—it is best to end the conversation by agreeing with her that she does not have to go. A battle of the wills usually just creates more tension and upsets both of you. If your loved one's cognitive limitations are significant enough that she needs an adult day care program, it is likely that after allowing some time to pass, she may forget her objections, and you can simply help her get ready to go to the program.

Shelley remembers many times when her father would become agitated over having to do something. If Shelley agreed with him and allowed a short period of time to elapse, she could then, usually, encourage him to do what he had just refused. The important part of this technique is to keep the environment calm and without confrontation.

If neither of these techniques works, talk to the staff at the adult day care program. They are skilled in working with people with cognitive limitations and will likely be able to help you find effective ways to encourage your loved one to attend.

My coworker at school knew my mother was going through so much with my father's dementia. She had an aunt who attended an adult day care program, and she told me how it worked. I was amazed to learn that there were places like that. I felt so bad for Mom, spending her whole day with Dad, never getting away from the responsibility of caring for him. I called the county senior services organization, and sure enough, there was a center just a few miles away.

It was hard for Mom to think about dropping Dad off and leaving him there. We talked a lot about her guilty feelings, but that she was so tired and worn out having him at home all the time. Finally, Mom and I went to visit the center. It was wonderful to see all these people occupied in group activities and interacting with a helpful staff. Mom was relieved, and we knew it would be a safe and helpful place.

Dad didn't seem to like it at first so we backed off. Then, about a week later, we tried again. This time he

was much less agitated. The staff said to go slowly, but
to keep bringing him back. Mom did, and in a few weeks
Dad began to look forward to going; sometimes he was
out the front door before Mom was ready herself.
I feel so pleased that we were able to find this
respite care. I can see a change for the better in Mom
and Dad both. Sometimes, I see a spark in him I haven't
seen in a while. The stimulation at the center has been
a gift to us all.

Mariellen, 42

Plans A, B, and Even C

College graduates often hear the advice that success is being prepared with Plan B. In caregiving, we know that even Plan B may not be enough to insure success. It quickly becomes obvious that we need to have plans and backup plans and backup, backup plans for the myriad situations that can occur as we care for our loved ones.

Plan A includes the normal assistance and supplies needed to care for your loved one. You are probably a very organized person, and you schedule your days as much as possible to make sure that medications and supplies are available.

Plan B prepares for situations that arise despite your careful planning. You need to be prepared to handle these with as little stress as possible. Here are some examples:

► Plan A: You've arranged for professional caregiving or nursing assistance for your loved one while you are away from home. Then, the professional caregiver you're counting on calls in sick. Now what?

Plan B: Register with a home care agency so you will have a resource for backup care from a qualified professional.

Plan C: Preregister with a second agency in case the first does not have a caregiver or nurse available for that shift.

▶ Plan A: Order medical supplies and prescription medicines before your loved one's supply runs out.

Plan B: Unforeseeable circumstances can cause the medicine or supplies to be delayed. Have insurance approvals and doctor's authorizations on file, and never delay having prescriptions refilled or ordered.

Plan C: Make sure you can get all necessary supplies and medications locally.

▶ A common caregiver fear is: what would happen if I got sick?

Plan A: Because your ability to provide care is impacted if you become ill, it is critical that you focus on your own health first. This includes eating right, getting adequate sleep, and having regular medical checkups. Regular medical care may seem particularly difficult since you spend so much time around doctors already.

Plan B: When you do get too sick to care for your loved one, have at least one relative or friend, or an agency person, who can commit to be your backup.

Plan C: Call for an extra backup from friends or professionals in case your first one cannot make it that day. Be ready to admit that the sub will not give care in the same manner you do. We all work differently, but it doesn't mean your loved one will not be well cared for.

It may seem that having one caregiving plan is difficult enough, much less two or three. However, careful planning with backup plans can eliminate a great deal of the stress as unexpected situations present themselves.

―⁂―

I certainly thought I had all bases covered when Jack was diagnosed with metastatic cancer. He had to go through a rigorous course of chemotherapy for more than four months. Unfortunately, I learned the hard way that when my daughter got caught in her own family crisis, I was pretty much left on my own to supply all home and transportation needs. My supervisor was sympathetic but obviously did not want me to be out every day for several hours.

So my organizational skills were put to the test. I lined up several friends who could commit to take Jack to and from the hospital. They each had the phone numbers of the others, so no one would feel too much pressure if something came up.

I contacted two agencies and registered for backup home care with both. I placed one as the primary and arranged for home coverage during each day when Jack got home from treatment.

I noticed that I began to feel calmer and less burdened. I don't know why I thought my daughter and I had to cover everything ourselves. I suppose I was in some kind of denial about Jack's needs and, therefore, how serious the cancer was. I think Jack is feeling more relaxed knowing I have help.

Now I see myself as proactive. I make sure all his medications are refilled a week before they run out. I have a list, right by the phone, of people I can call in the night if I need some help with Jack, as well as all emergency numbers if it is something more serious.

"Expect the unexpected" is a helpful motto when you are a caregiver. When you think you have covered all your bases, check again; you'll be glad you did.

Cecile, 60

CHAPTER SEVEN

Caregiving as a Transformational Experience

*He who has gone, so we but cherish his
memory, abides with us, more potent, nay,
more present than the living man.*

ANTOINE DE SAINT-EXUPÉRY

A MAJOR THEME OF THIS BOOK is that caregiving can be a transformational experience: forever changing our perspectives, and therefore our lives. In this chapter I talk about some of the ways we are transformed by caregiving. You will read articles and stories that discuss how we let our loved ones go, and at the same time keep them alive and honor them in our memories. There are also articles and stories to help you prevent regrets and to release regrets you already have.

Through the ideas presented in the articles and stories in this chapter, and throughout the book, I hope you find ways to make caregiving transformational in your own life. I hope you find ways to emerge from this experience with a deeper realization of what really matters in life and how to have more of that on a day to day basis. Those are the greatest gifts anyone can take from their caregiving journey, and I wish those gifts for you.

Living in Suspended Animation

Have you ever had the feeling that your life was on hold? That you are living in a sort of suspended animation? Long-term caregiving can make you feel that you are not where you used to be, but yet not where you are going to be, either. You may feel like the cartoon character with the perpetual cloud over his head. For caregivers, this could be a cloud of anxiety and uncertainty.

Rather than accepting a life on hold, try to live your life, right now, as a caregiver. You were not a caregiver in the past, and there will probably come a time when you will not be a caregiver again. But for now, this *is* your life. The Bible reminds us that everything has its own season, or time: "a time to be born, a time to die; a time to cry, a time to laugh; a time to mourn, a time to dance..." (Ecclesiastes 3:1–8).

Mitch sometimes thought about what his life would be like when his ill wife passed away. Then he'd feel guilty thinking how much easier his life would be when he no longer had caregiving responsibilities. In fact, having those thoughts actually helped prepare Mitch for his future without his wife. He was able to speak with her, gently, about her passing and her wishes, as well as to talk about the emotional aspects of their relationship. He was able to tell his wife how much he would miss her.

Mitch learned that his wife preferred cremation, something he had not known. She asked that her ashes be taken to her parents' farm, where she was raised. She shared her child-hood memories of roaming the pastures with the animals, walking with her dog as he herded the cows in for milking. This brought such peace to Mitch. He knew his wife's wishes and took great comfort in seeing her at rest in a place that held significance for her.

Many conversations followed as Mitch and his wife shared their own memories. She told him how much she appreciated his taking care of her through the illness. Mitch recorded a CD of their favorite music interspersed with his own voice talking about each song. Mitch's wife kept that music playing softly through her last days.

Your caregiving experience is part of your own life cycle, not a life on hold, but rather, a life flow.

—◦◦◦◦◦—

The main thing I've learned from the many changes that have happened in my life is that I just can't hurry the process. I remember when I left home to go to college, I spent the first few months thinking about how much I missed my family and friends at home. It took me a while to begin to get involved in college life and get to know my roommates and professors. I remember feeling as though I was just hovering above the experience. I knew I would be okay when I finally said to myself—it's okay to be just where you are, in the midst of a big life change.

Now that I am taking care of my dad in his final days, I try to remind myself that I can't have him the way he used to be. I don't know what life will be like when he dies. So I need to concentrate on what is happening now and make the most of the time we have together. Even though Dad is severely limited in what he can do and say, we can still make this time very special for both of us.

Mike, 47

A Trip Down Memory Lane

When a loved one is critically ill, it is easy to spend your waking hours talking about medical issues and the logistics of getting all the things done that need doing. We can become too comfortable, settling into conversations around that single topic. Instead of talking about doctors and medicine and illness, take your loved one on a trip down memory lane. You may want to ask other family members and friends to join you. It is a quick and easy way to switch the scene from gloom to joy and gratitude. You might even say *no regrets allowed*, except perhaps to say how you might do it differently the next time around.

You and your loved may decide to write down your conversations or even record them to share with other family and friends who are not nearby. What a lovely way to share these precious memories. You might do just a few minutes of reminiscing each day at a certain time or as the mood strikes. Even folks with memory problems may still be able to talk, with a bit of prompting, about what they remember. Here are some ideas for prompts to get you started.

► What was it like growing up in your hometown?

► What is the best thing that ever happened to you?

► What is the funniest thing?

► How about the worst thing?

► What do you wish you had known when you were younger?

► Who are some of the people you're grateful to? Why those people?

These memories are sure to give you lots to talk about for weeks to come. They can create more laughs than a funny video or CD.

Author Madeleine L'Engle said, "The great thing about getting older is that you don't lose all the other ages you have been." You have the wonderful opportunity to learn about all your loved one's other ages.

I have heard from many of my friends how much they regret not having a record of the stories their parents told. I always seem to be too busy to listen to my parents' memories and to encourage them to tell us more. Yet I've had this nagging feeling that I would be sorry if my parents died and their stories were lost.

So, my family and I set aside just a half hour a week on Sunday evenings after dinner. My son set up the recording system for us. My job was to think of questions to ask my parents to get them started reminiscing.

We all loved the experience. Now that Dad has died, Mom and all of us really enjoy listening to those recordings and laughing and crying together.

Jean, 57

Regrets

Caregivers sometimes feel regret about not having said or done something for their loved one. Once the loved one has died, these feelings may cause a good deal of emotional pain.

The irony of these feelings is that we can only experience them because we have grown and changed. Our perspective shifts as we age, and we look back through the eyes of experience, wisdom, compassion, and a deeper understanding about human difficulties.

Sometimes we experience regret because, for example, a circumstance shifts and we discover we have waited too long to take an action that later we wished we had taken.

How can we minimize regrets?

One way to do so is to live as consciously as possible. This means aligning our values, the outcomes we desire, and our actions. When Claire's mother had a serious stroke, Claire asked herself what type of caregiver she wanted to be; how did she want to look back on this time with her mother? Claire rearranged things in her life to fit that vision.

Determining the outcomes you want and living your values isn't always easy, but the rewards can be immeasurable. For example, when you face decisions, you can make them more quickly and confidently when you behave in accordance with your values and take the actions most likely to lead to the outcomes you desire.

Often just telling someone how we wished it had been different is helpful. Sometimes, though, it is too late to talk; we often gain our wisdom after someone has died and we can't directly share our feelings with them.

Anne's heart was so heavy with unspoken thoughts after her father died that she decided to have a conversation with him anyway. She sat in her father's garden in the early morning and expressed her feelings. We don't know if she spoke with her voice or with her heart, but it didn't matter. She knew her father so well that she could guess how he would respond to her feelings of regret. Anne knew she was being harder on herself than her father would have ever been, and imagining his responses reminded her of that.

Not everyone is comfortable with an imaginary conversation. After your loved one has died, you might prefer to talk with someone else whom both you and your loved one knew. By sharing your feelings with someone who knew you both, you'll have the benefit of a different perspective on what your loved one's likely response would have been.

Feelings of regret are usually a sign that you've grown and changed emotionally. You can acknowledge both the feelings of regret and the ways in which they signify your areas of emotional growth. Then you can turn your sights on releasing the regret and retaining the wisdom.

*I had real regrets after Laney died from breast cancer.
Her last year was very hard. We had hospice care for the last month, and that
was a big help to me. I thought at the time I was doing
everything I could for her, but I knew I wasn't really
talking to her in a way that showed my feelings.
I went through a very bad time, beating myself up
about all the things I did not do. Hospice introduced me
to a bereavement group, and I was relieved to know I
wasn't the only one feeling regret and guilt. I talked
with friends who knew Laney well. My golf buddy
said that he and his wife thought I did a great job.
Laney had told them both what wonderful care I
was giving her.
I now believe I gave her my love and caring, and
I did it the best way I could. I miss her, but my sad
regrets have faded. I try now to remember all our
great times together.*

Frank, 70

What's It All About?

Danish philosopher Sören Keirkegaard said, "Life can only be
understood backwards, but it must be lived forwards." You may
get glimpses from time to time of the big picture of your loved
one's illness, of your caregiving and what it means to both of
you. It may take years after your caregiving has ended for the
entire experience to really sink in.

Some caregivers want to try to *look* as well as *live* forwards
and make sense of the experience while it was happening.

Mary felt lucky for the experience of helping her father
make the most of his final years. She did not just sit by idly

waiting for his illness to progress; rather, she decided to do at least one thing each day to make her father feel good about himself. They weren't complicated or difficult things. Mary and her father talked about his experience during World War II and the time he met Mary's mother. He directed Mary how to replace the light fixture over the kitchen table and to check the oil in the car. It gave them both joy and a sense of accomplishment.

Andrew never found it easy to express his feelings toward his grandmother. He feared that when she passed away, he'd regret having struggled to say, "I love you." He started by simply telling his grandmother how much he'd always loved visiting her and looked forward to having some of her special blackberry jam. The words, and emotion, began to flow more easily as he thanked her for things she and his grandfather had taught him. Andrew even mustered the courage to apologize for boyhood pranks and thoughtlessness. He saw how touched his grandmother was, which softened him as well.

Ellis often wondered what he did to deserve this caregiving responsibility for his dad. His wife, who believed everything happens for a reason, suggested that perhaps Ellis had something to learn. Maybe caring for his father was a blessing in disguise. She told Ellis she'd already seen him become a more patient person, and how being in the midst of his father's health crisis had made him more aware of the importance of maintaining his own health. His priorities had clearly shifted, putting family concerns ahead of work.

If you are tempted to ask yourself what this caregiving experience is all about, step back and take a look at the big picture. This is a special time of blessings for you and others you may touch in your life.

—⚬⚬⚬—

I have to admit I got pretty caught up in feeling sorry
for myself since I agreed to take care of Aunt Gilda as

she battled lung cancer. The worst part was I felt like I was beginning to take my frustration out on her with mean remarks, even though I loved her dearly.

I knew it was time for an attitude adjustment, so I asked my brother to take over the caregiving and I went to the beach for the weekend. I spent hours remembering all the wonderful times I spent with Aunt Gilda when I was a kid. Then I thought about the present situation, and I asked myself, during all the giving, what can I take from this experience?

I came home feeling refreshed and recharged. I told Aunt Gilda how grateful I was to have this opportunity to spend time with her. I know now that this experience has boosted my ability to express love and gratitude and even patience.

Betty, 52

The Messiness of Grief

Caregivers are often surprised by how alone and empty they feel when their loved one dies. They don't feel the expected relief, even following a long and difficult time of caregiving. It doesn't matter whether the death is expected or unexpected, prolonged or sudden. The caregiver may think he or she has grieved along the way—was somehow prepared for the death—but grief may still surge to new heights after the loved one dies.

There are many theories about how people grieve. Many people are familiar with the stages of grief described by psychiatrist Dr. Elisabeth Kübler-Ross. They are denial, anger, bargaining, depression, and resolution. While it may sound very orderly, emotions don't usually fit into a neat list. Try as we might, we cannot usually control when emotions surface or how long they stay.

You have probably experienced grief and loss in your life and so you understand the concept, at least intellectually. But with time, you release the grief and your heart forgets just how messy it was, how it felt absolutely overwhelming one moment and then lifted slightly in the next. You might be months past your loved one's death and feeling as though you are regaining your emotional equilibrium when, *bang*, you are hit by another wave of grief that sends you crashing downward again.

Florence and Evelyn, members of a bereavement group, agreed that it is simply exhausting to grieve. This was especially true during the period immediately following the loved one's death. It was all they could do to make it through the day's routine. Florence felt there was not enough space or time to grieve. Friends and family expected her to get over the loss and back to living her old, *normal* life. Both women knew that what they really needed was to take some time off just to grieve.

As anyone who has suffered a major loss knows, that old, *normal* life no longer exists. Instead, a new normal emerges, one that integrates your loved one through memories and stories and traditions carried forward. This carrying forward is both your loved one's gift to you and your gift to him or her.

Although grief is messy, unpredictable, exhausting, and nearly impossible to control, it does offer benefits. We never again see life in quite the same way. Our perspective on life is almost always changed, and we begin to focus on the things that really matter.

—◦◦◦—

When Gordon died, I thought I was ready. He had been sick for a long time. We had been able to have many conversations and shared good memories together before his mental capacity began to deteriorate. I thought that we had even done a good deal of grieving with each other.

So I was amazed when, about a month after his death, I became terribly angry and would cry for long periods of time. I began to avoid seeing my friends and would not answer the phone. My children were worried and spoke with my family physician. They learned, and helped me see, that grieving can take many forms.

My daughter suggested that I might be trying to do too much, because I was really tired all the time. So I cut back on planning some social activities, and limited myself to one event per day. This has helped, and I feel a little more energized.

I still get angry and sometimes depressed, but now I know it is all tied to my connection to my beloved Gordon. I am only human, after all, and not able to make this process a neat, little package. I know I will go through these stages not feeling in control, but I do have those wonderful memories with Gordon and I wouldn't want it any other way.

Norah, 76

How Old Was He?

It is often hard for people to know just how to offer comfort when someone has lost a loved one. A usual comment is, "...well, he lived a good, long life," which carries the suggestion that is was time for him to go. Small comfort for the bereaved family.

Anita was very close to her aunt and uncle and was one of their caregivers. Her uncle's death was very difficult for her. She was dumbfounded when people asked how old he was, then, learning he was in his late eighties, said something about how he is better off, is at peace, or is no longer suffering. For Anita, the comments implied that she shouldn't feel sad about her uncle's death because he was old. She had lost a very important person in her life, even though he was old when he died. She vowed never to ask the age of the person who died or suggest the loved one is better off, because it simply does not matter to those who are grieving.

Joseph grieved deeply after his mother died at the age of 99. Regardless of her age, she was Joseph's mother, and he no longer had her with him.

How, then, do you respond to people who say such things? Remembering the intention is probably to offer comfort and support, you might respond with a comment that is gentle, appreciative, and, hopefully, helps educate the person about the nature of loss. You might say something like:

- ► Thank you for your thoughts. He was such an important part of my life and I'm very sad he is gone. I am glad he got to live such a good, long life, but the fact he was old doesn't make me miss him any less.

- ► Thank you for your thoughts. You know, I thought it might easier for me because he was so old when he died. But I've realized that the age doesn't matter. All that really matters is that I've have lost someone I loved dearly.

We can't always predict what people will say or how we'll react to their comments. It's important, though, to express your feelings honestly, especially in a time of bereavement. A response that is kind and appreciative, and also serves to educate the person about your feelings, may help you during the sad period of grieving.

I always found it hard to know what to say to someone who has lost a dear one. My approach is basically to say less rather than more, usually just telling them that I am sorry for their loss and hope I can help them in some way.

*When my husband died recently after a long,
painful bout with cancer, I received many lovely cards
from people expressing their sorrow and support.
However, there were a few cards that I know were sent
by people with all good intentions, but I just didn't like
the message. They stressed what a blessing it was that
he had died, so he could end his suffering and mine.
Maybe at some later time I will feel that sense of blessing, but right now I feel only the loss and I would give
anything to have my husband back with me. I don't
think people should try to assume they know what I'm
feeling or make judgments about my husband's death.*

Robin, 76

Mother's Day

Mother's Day can evoke many emotions. Holidays, birthdays, and other special days often trigger memories of times past and serve as a sometimes sad reminder that some people and things will never be part of our lives again.

If your mother has passed on recently, you may still be reeling from the loss. The first Mother's Day after a mother's death is often the hardest, but the feeling of loss on that day may not go away even years later. These special days often evoke what is called a *STUG* reaction, or a *sudden temporary upsurge of grief.* These temporary grief reactions are frequently triggered by holidays and other memorable events, and their depth often takes people by surprise. These upsurges, though, are almost always temporary.

Mother's Day is a hard day for Margaret to endure. She takes care of her mother, who is frail and has dementia, and Margaret knows her mother will probably not live for many more years. She finds herself grateful for the time with her mother and, at the same time, grieving the loss of the strong, robust mother who raised her. She sees a future Mother's Day with no one to celebrate.

Some caregivers are embarrassed by these sad emotions because they don't believe they are logical. They think it crazy to be grieving for a mother who is sitting right beside them or to wish a suffering loved one would not die. While these feelings may not seem logical, they are anything but crazy. We cannot control how and when feelings appear, and it may be best just to acknowledge and experience them rather than try to explain or justify them.

Whether your mother is living or dead, whether you had a wonderful or a painful relationship, it is normal to have mixed feelings on Mother's Day. And, as usually happens, you will likely find that the intensity of those feelings will lessen and you will regain your sense of emotional equilibrium.

Advantages of getting older are the accompanying life experience and the resulting wisdom. We recognize that whatever is happening at this moment will soon change, and life will continue to bring new and different experiences. Some of the wisdom is accepting the loss of things past. We don't need to dwell on loss or become paralyzed by it, but we might pause every so often and silently acknowledge the people and experiences that came before. So whether your mother is living or dead, you can tip your hat to her and feel whatever emotions arise.

—◦◦◦—

I took care of my mother during the last six months of her life, and I am so grateful that I had the chance to get to know her in a whole new way. We had quite a rocky relationship when I was young, because we had such different personalities. She was a stable force in all our lives, a stay-at-home mom who cooked and cleaned and took care of four children. I, on the other hand, was the family dreamer, often forgetting to do my chores and homework.

Although Mom tried to get me to tow the line, I really gave her a hard time and many sleepless nights. I ran off to Hollywood to be an actress when I was just 17 and never looked back. Mom came to accept my life choices. She was proud of me when I got a good part in a show, and she commiserated when I was rejected.

When Mom was diagnosed with liver cancer, I knew I needed to be with her for those last days. I took a break from my acting career and came home to live with her.

We talked about my career and my life, and then I asked her questions about her dreams and plans when she was a young woman. My biggest surprise was to learn that Mom had actually wanted to go into the theater herself, but she met my dad and the rest was history. She did have some regrets, although she had loved her life as wife and mother. She admitted that she lived her dream through me and my life as an actress.

Mom is gone now, but I think of her every day, and when Mother's Day rolls around, I toast Mom and dreams fulfilled.

Stella, 52

Father's Day

For many of us, our fathers were among the first caregivers in our lives. Not everyone has the perfect relationship with his or her father; instead, relationships with our parent are often very complex. Holidays like Father's Day are often reminders of this complexity, regardless of whether our fathers are living or dead.

Even if your relationship with your father was more strained than harmonious, it is likely that it will stand as one of the most important relationships in your life. And it is likely that no matter what the quality of your relationship is, or was, with your father, there are wonderful life lessons, stories, and memories that will stay with you throughout your life. You can choose today to reflect on and honor all that you have learned from your father, all the ways your father has positively shaped your life. Here are some points to ponder.

► How did my father help me become the person I am today?

► How did he shape my values, my path in life?

► What did I learn from my father?

► What qualities does (did) my father have that I value and respect?

► What are some of my favorite stories about my father?

► What are some of my happiest memories of my father?

► What stories about my father, memories about my father, things my father taught me, do I want to pass on to my own children?

If your father is still living, take the opportunity to share with him some of your positive memories. It will likely be one of the greatest gifts he will ever receive. Most parents wish they had done some things differently and feel, in hindsight, they could have been better parents. Your father would, no doubt, take great pleasure in hearing about the things that you thought he did well.

It is partly by retelling old stories that we keep people's memories alive. If your father has passed on, perhaps reflecting on these points will help you feel your father's presence with you in your life today.

Whether your father is healthy, frail, suffering with cognitive challenges, or no longer with you, you can pause and acknowledge him.

I remind myself that I only have one father, so on special days—Father's Day, birthdays, holidays—I think about Dad, his strengths and his shortcomings.

Of course, I have regrets about my own behavior. When my dad became ill, I didn't realize how serious it was, and I didn't get home for a few weeks. Yet I am always grateful that we had his last six weeks together, to talk, to reminisce, and to say how much we matter to each other. The values and integrity that he passed on to me are always there. Even though I am not conscious of it, I know there is a part of him that is inside me, helping me choose a certain path.

I try to remember stories he told me of his childhood, and I am so glad when a story that I had forgotten for a while flies back to me. These memories are treasures that I will pass on in whatever way I can.

Jeremy, 62

No One Loves You Like Your Mother Does

A caregiver whose mother had died eight months before said she was shocked by how much her mother's death had impacted her life. Caregivers may assume that after a brief period of grief they can release it and return to their everyday lives. What often happens, though, is that we are gripped, unexpectedly, by the grief, and little things remind us of our loved ones. Sometimes we're embarrassed by the level of grief or think that what we're experiencing is not normal.

When your mother dies there seems to be a special grief that you experience. But consider the connection we have with our mothers even before we are born. Mothers provide our first home and nourish us so that we can begin our lives. The bond between mothers and their children is uniquely strong even in the face of enormous difficulties.

Possibly the best way we support a caregiver whose mother has passed on is simply to acknowledge how difficult it is. Fred, a physician, said he only recently realized that he was mildly depressed for about a year and a half after his mother died. He said, "No one ever tells you how hard it is to lose your mother—regardless of your age or hers."

The grief, though, doesn't maintain its intensity forever, just longer than many people think it will. If you do find that your grief is interfering with your ability to function, don't hesitate to talk to a mental health professional who has the skill and experience to help you move through the grief.

It is good to be aware that even after the intense grief has ended you will sometimes find yourself caught off-guard by a strong feeling of sadness, often triggered by a memory or a holiday. These moments of sadness may occur occasionally for the rest of your life. It may help if you reframe them as signs of your deep connection with your mother.

Losing someone you love is never easy. Losing your mother is especially difficult. So honor and allow the feelings as a sign of the bond you had with your mother.

—⸺⸺⸺—

I've been thinking lately about the whole notion of unconditional love and trying to figure out if it really exists. Many spouses and friends certainly have special love relationships as do siblings and family. But the love of a mother for her child comes as close to being unconditional as we can get. I know that was true with my mother. Still, it doesn't mean we agreed on every-thing, but no matter how tense things got, I knew that Mom loved me. She had a way of always seeing my point of view and standing up for me when needed.

Probably the truest sign of her love was as I grew to adulthood. Mom maintained a role that helped to keep open communication through the years, and she encouraged me to do the same as my own children grew. Mom always said she was a guide on the side, not a sage on the stage. She was there to catch me when I fell, both literally and figuratively, but she never tried to prevent me from trying the things that might make me fall.

Sally, 64

Remembering Our Parents

Our relationships with our parents are ever evolving. In the beginning the parent is caregiver to the child. As time passes, the child relies less on his parent for nurturing and care. However, well into adulthood, nurturing still seems to flow in one direction: parent to child.

The child may become a caregiver to the parent and the nurturing flows more from the child to the parent than the parent to the child. The caregiver now has new responsibilities and often misses the parental nurturing.

If you have been caring for a parent whose physical or mental health has been fading for some time, you may fear that when he or she dies, your only memories will be of this difficult time. In fact, the memories that linger longest are the fond ones.

Even if, like many people's, your relationship with your parent was complex and sometimes difficult, you are apt to remember the positive things about your parent and the good things the relationship brought into your life. Most people will recall memories when their loved one was happy and healthy.

It took Phil a little time to bring back the good memories after his mother passed away. Things his mother had told him as a child came back slowly; she always knew just what would interest him. When Phil was young, his mother recognized that he needed an emotional outlet and encouraged him in drama and theater work. She sang songs to him that he can now recall, hearing her voice in his mind. These warm memories continued to comfort Phil and lessened the sad memories of his mother's illness and passing.

My mother and I did not have an easy relationship. There was love, but it was not easily expressed by either of us. After my father's death, my mother seemed to recede into another world. I tried very hard to make her life as comfortable as was possible. It just seemed that nothing worked that well and when she died, I felt like I'd been a disappointment.

It took me a little time to bring back the good memories; they came back slowly. I began to recall things my mother told me as a child that she knew would interest me. I remember how she sang to me on the porch swing when it was so dark and cold. I can still hear her voice. Her love was apparent, but I was too young to recognize it.

I wish we had talked more in her last years. For me now, bringing back the good memories is my way of talking with her. I truly appreciate and respect the woman she was. I feel sure she knows that.

Martha, 56
